# The Bible and the Brain

*Where He Leads Me,*
*I Will Follow*

*The Bible and the Brain: Where He Leads Me, I Will Follow*

A *FocusChoice Therapy* publication.

Copyright © 2017 by David C. Heebner. All rights reserved.

Please visit **www.focuschoicetherapy.com** for more about David Heebner's new and innovative therapy model, information about products and services, and to order additional copies of this title or David's other books.

David C. Heebner, LPC

14143 Robert Paris Court
Chantilly, Virginia 20151

43129 Tall Pines Court
Ashburn, Virginia 20147

ISBN: 1542342112
ISBN-13: 978-1542342117

All Scripture quotations in this publication are from THE MESSAGE. Copyright © by Eugene H. Peterson 1993, 1994, 1995, 1996, 2000, 2001, 2002. Used by permission of NavPress. All rights reserved. Represented by Tyndale House Publishers, Inc.

*Cover design: Qinisile Nkosi, Chris Eberly*
*Interior design: Chris Eberly*
*Editors: Chris Eberly, Deborah Gonzalez*

*Printed in the United States of America.*

# Contents

About the Cover ................................................................. i
Forward ............................................................................. iii
Introduction ....................................................................... v
How to Use This Book .................................................... ix

Your Thoughts Sculpt Your Brain ................................... 2
Five Senses, One Focus .................................................. 4
Renewal at the Cellular Level ......................................... 6
Making the Right Choice ................................................ 8
Faulty Thinking ............................................................... 12
Through a New Lens ....................................................... 14
Abnormally Positive Psychology .................................... 16
…and the Pursuit of Happiness ....................................... 18
Something Bigger Than Yourself .................................... 22
God Has a Plan ................................................................ 24
The Happy Quitter ........................................................... 26
Spreading the Good News ............................................... 28
Our Failure at Self-change .............................................. 30
No Help Needed .............................................................. 32
Keep Your Eyes on Jesus ................................................ 34
God's Truth Permeates All .............................................. 36
God is Creator of Life and Happiness ............................. 40
God's House of Thoughts ................................................ 42
Fill Your Mind with the Best .......................................... 46
High on God ..................................................................... 48
Great Sensory Escapes .................................................... 50
Nowhere Else to Turn ...................................................... 52
Old Barns Made New ...................................................... 56
Trust .................................................................................. 58
Faith, Hope, and Trust ..................................................... 60
A New Normal ................................................................. 64
Living in Rhythm with God ............................................ 68
To Rest Is To Work .......................................................... 70
Rest in God's Garden ....................................................... 72

| | |
|---|---|
| A Circle of Angels | 74 |
| Getting into the Zone | 78 |
| Use Your Passion | 82 |
| Embrace Every Moment in God | 84 |
| Become a Slave and Be Set Free | 86 |
| Sitting at God's Feet | 88 |
| Understanding and Embracing Fear | 92 |
| The Joy of the Lord is My Strength | 94 |
| Our Thoughts are Crazy! | 96 |
| Our Work is Easy | 98 |
| Unconditional Love | 102 |
| Everyone Has a Plan | 104 |
| God Doesn't Think Like Us | 108 |
| Whose Voice Do You Hear? | 110 |
| God's Voice is Not Anxious | 112 |
| The Problem Solver | 114 |
| Easy Times | 116 |
| A Divine Think Tank | 120 |
| Turn Your Eyes Upon Jesus | 122 |
| Our Addiction of Choice | 126 |
| Thought Addiction | 128 |
| A Thought Transfusion | 130 |
| God's Computer in Us | 132 |
| Even Me | 134 |
| Wear Love | 136 |
| Living in the Freedom of God | 138 |
| Pass along the Gift of God's Love | 140 |
| Don't Give Your Thoughts a Vote | 142 |
| God's Strong, Gentle Voice | 146 |
| God's Safe-House | 150 |
| A Basket of Stress | 152 |
| God, You've Done It All! | 156 |
| Living in Bondage | 158 |
| He Calls His Sheep by Name | 160 |
| The Gift of Sensory Focus | 162 |
| Our Bondage of Cursed Thinking | 164 |

| | |
|---|---|
| Starting Over as Children | 166 |
| Growing Up in Christ | 170 |
| Our Own Twisted Thinking | 172 |
| God's Grace is Enough | 174 |
| Losing Control | 178 |
| The Power of Love | 180 |
| Hard Times | 184 |
| God's Love, Delivered Fresh Daily | 188 |
| Be Alert! | 190 |
| Snowdrifts of Thoughts | 192 |
| The Extravagant Dimensions of God's Love | 194 |
| Flip the Switch to God | 196 |
| The Wind in My Sails | 200 |
| Hitting Bottom | 202 |
| Our Backs Turned to God | 204 |
| Going Through Hard Times | 206 |
| Once Upon a Time | 208 |
| God Made Our Mind to See | 210 |
| Don't Argue with God | 212 |
| Stop Thinking! | 214 |
| Stop Trying So Hard | 216 |
| God's Love is Electric | 218 |
| God Lives in Us | 222 |
| Don't Worry | 224 |
| Raised from the Dead | 226 |
| What a Surprise | 228 |
| You Don't Have to Listen to Sin | 230 |
| | |
| References | 234 |
| Scripture Index | 236 |
| About the Author | 241 |

# *About the Cover*

*By your words I can see where I'm going;
   they throw a beam of light on my dark path.*
(Psalm 119:105)

*Jesus once again addressed them: "I am the world's Light. No one who follows me stumbles around in the darkness. I provide plenty of light to live in."*
(John 8:12)

*The Life-Light blazed out of the darkness;
   the darkness couldn't put it out.*

*There once was a man, his name John, sent by God to point out the way to the Life-Light. He came to show everyone where to look, who to believe in. John was not himself the Light; he was there to show the way to the Light.*

*The Life-Light was the real thing:
   Every person entering Life
   he brings into Light.* (John 1:5-9)

*"No one lights a lamp, then hides it in a drawer. It's put on a lamp stand so those entering the room have light to see where they're going. Your eye is a lamp, lighting up your whole body."* (Luke 11:33-34)

Our eyes (in fact, all five of our senses) are our lamp. This sensory focus on God is how we enter the room to God's love. The sensory side of our brain is the receiving center for everything God has to say to us and give us. Our continual, conscious choice to keep our eyes on him is exactly how the light bulb is on for God to live in and through us.

The light that shines through reading the Bible supercharges the neurotransmitters in our brain. Learning about how God made the brain has shed new light on the exact meaning of what God has in scripture. At times, this meaning is upside down or exactly the opposite of what I used to think it meant.

# *Forward*

*But I need something more! For if I know the law but still can't keep it, and if the power of sin within me keeps sabotaging my best intentions, I obviously need help! I realize that I don't have what it takes. I can will it, but I can't do it. I decide to do good, but I don't really do it; I decide not to do bad, but then I do it anyway. My decisions, such as they are, don't result in actions. Something has gone wrong deep within me and gets the better of me every time.*

*It happens so regularly that it's predictable. The moment I decide to do good, sin is there to trip me up. I truly delight in God's commands, but it's pretty obvious that not all of me joins in that delight. Parts of me covertly rebel, and just when I least expect it, they take charge.*

*I've tried everything and nothing helps. I'm at the end of my rope. Is there no one who can do anything for me? Isn't that the real question?*

*The answer, thank God, is that Jesus Christ can and does. He acted to set things right in this life of contradictions where I want to serve God with all my heart and mind, but am pulled by the influence of sin to do something totally different.* (Romans 7:17-25)

Scripture verses like these were so instrumental in my decision to let God take over running my life. I have not been able to contain my joy! I went from feeling so bad to feeling so good about how much God loves me. I want to share everything God shows me. Every time I read The Bible (I like The Message translation by Eugene Peterson) I feel so happy because God shares so many words with me to put into writing. He does the same thing as I keep finding more research on how God made our brain. For me, this sensory time with God—where I read and write about what God wants to teach me—has saved me from a life of depression.

It's not like learning how God made the brain changes what the Bible says. It simply opened my eyes to the real meaning of what the Bible teaches. So often we take an opposite or upside down meaning of what his Word tells us because we falsely believe the brain is made backwards from God's actual design.

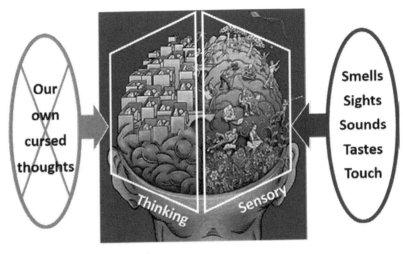

God is in the ongoing process of transforming my life into his likeness. Putting the thoughts and words that God shares with me into book form is simply my way of sharing this transformation with everyone. In fact, all the books I am writing for FocusChoice Therapy Publications are, first and foremost, my simple way of sharing with my clients, with pastors and Christian Counselors, and readers all over the world how God has literally saved my life.

# *Introduction*

I attended Eastern Mennonite University in Harrisonburg, Virginia (perhaps better known for being the home of the other college in town, James Madison University). We were required to attend Chapel every day. One morning during the chapel service, my cousin, David Seitz, sang a secular song by Simon and Garfunkel, "Bridge Over Troubled Water" (Columbia Records, 1970). My cousin, a music professor at the school, raised some eyebrows with this "hippie" song. Yes, I admit I wore "bell-bottoms" in college. Recently, I was singing the song and the lyrics inspired me to write this book, *The Bible and the Brain*. Here are the first two verses:

> When you're weary, feeling small
> When tears are in your eyes, I'll dry them all
> I'm on your side, oh, when times get rough
> And friends just can't be found
> Like a bridge over troubled water
> I will lay me down
> Like a bridge over troubled water
> I will lay me down
>
> When you're down and out
> When you're on the street
> When evening falls so hard
> I will comfort you
> I'll take your part, oh, when darkness comes
> And pain is all around
> Like a bridge over troubled water
> I will lay me down
> Like a bridge over troubled water
> I will lay me down

God wants to lay himself down for us all the time. He is on our side. He wants to dry our tears and comfort us through rough times. He offers to take our part. Such true and beautiful words! So many people whose hearts are breaking want to be rescued. They feel so worn out and weary. They just want so badly to rest. From Matthew 11:28:

*"Are you tired? Worn out? Burned out on religion? Come to me. Get away with me and you'll recover your life. I'll show you how to take a real rest."*

How do we come to him? No one has ever really explained how, because no one ever knew how God designed our brain. Yet, in the next two verses (Matthew 11:29-30), God tells us exactly how to come to him:

*"Walk with me and work with me—watch how I do it. Learn the unforced rhythms of grace. I won't lay anything heavy or ill-fitting on you. Keep company with me and you'll learn to live freely and lightly."*

Even though these verses tell us to walk with God and watch him so we can learn the unforced rhythms of grace, I did not know exactly what those words meant until I learned how God made the brain.

The one word that jumped off the page at me from these last two verses is "rhythms". The meaning of this word became very powerful to me once I learned about God's brilliant design for our brain. Dr. Francine Shapiro, an American psychologist, made a chance observation as she was walking through Central Park in New York City in 1987. She was very stressed at the time. Suddenly two beautiful red robins caught her attention as they chased each other. As her eyes followed the robins darting back and forth, she noticed that her rapid eye movements from side to side quickly relieved her stress. Following this discovery, Dr. Shapiro developed EMDR (Eye Movement

Desensitization and Reprocessing), a form of psychotherapy for resolving the symptoms of traumatic and other disturbing life experiences.

Wow! God created our brain so that quickly moving our eyes laterally gives us instant relief from stress, faster than Xanax! Not only does rhythmic eye movement have an immediate relaxing effect but so does rhythmic action in our other four senses. Rhythmic touch, taste, smell and sound have the same wonderful effect. Why do you think God invented rocking chairs and music drums? Several years ago, a teenage client came to my office in severe distress. He could not stop worrying that the world was going to end on a certain date. He said absolutely nothing could distract him from his awful thoughts. I used an iPhone app called Magic Piano to switch his mind out of thinking mode and into sensory mode. The sounds, touch, motion, and colors of the song he played relaxed my client in no time at all.

By combining how God made the brain with the meaning of these verses in Matthew 11, God has clearly shown me how walking with him and watching him teaches us how to live freely and lightly. "Unforced rhythms" is a great description of how it takes no human mental effort whatsoever to keep our sensory focus on God. Simply make the continual, conscious choice to stay in constant prayer through rhythmic attention to God with one or more of our five senses. When we do, we have embraced the true meaning of getting away with God, keeping company with him, and recovering the life of happiness that God desires for all of us That was his original purpose with Adam and Eve. He simply wanted them to embrace the Garden of Eden with their five senses, and stay away from the tree of knowledge. Or as I like to say, the tree of STINKIN' THINKIN'.

# *How to Use This Book*

This book is not written in the traditional chapter format, with the customary 12-20 pages per chapter. The Bible and the Brain is written in brief sections intended to enlighten your mind in a progressive fashion as you progress through each section. It is written to have each reader begin to practice and put into action the technique of identifying God's thoughts as opposed to our own, from the very first section. Just from reading the introduction, the distinction between God's thoughts and my thoughts has already come into play even before reading these instructions. What is this distinction? God's thoughts are uplifting; mine are discouraging.

<u>Uplifting</u>
- Wow, what an amazing song to sing for God (Bridge Over Troubled Water)
- God made our brains to worship him

<u>Discouraging</u>
- What can a Mennonite boy who grew up on a dairy farm possibly offer?
- No one will read this book

As you read each section, please take a little time to journal God's uplifting thoughts versus your own discouraging ones. Do not attempt to figure out God's thoughts versus your own. There is nothing to figure out. If the though is positive, it goes on God's side; if it's negative, it goes on your side. By the end of the book, God will have enlightened you to the beautiful world of seeing life through his eyes.

# The Bible and the Brain

## *Your Thoughts Sculpt Your Brain*

The above title came from a section heading in an article by Debbie Hampton[1]. Within that section was the following text:

> One example of this is the well-known London cab driver studies[2] which showed that the longer someone had been driving a taxi, the larger their hippocampus, a part of the brain involved in visual-spatial memory. Their brains literally expanded to accommodate the cognitive demands of navigating London's tangle of streets.

How does this change occur? The same article described the physiological process:

> As a thought travels through your brain, neurons fire together in distinctive ways based on the information being handled, and those patterns of neural activity actually change your neural structure. Busy regions of the brain start making new connections with each other, and existing synapses, the connections between neurons, that experience more activity get stronger, increasingly sensitive, and start building more receptors. New synapses are also formed.

It is fascinating for me to learn how God completed the miracle of the human brain. For God to design our brain

| *Uplifting* | *Discouraging* |
|---|---|
| ➢ | ➢ |
| ➢ | ➢ |
| ➢ | ➢ |

to be continually and dynamically upgraded is even more magnificent than the frequent upgrades applied to our laptops and cell phones. What is even more fascinating is that God told us about his continual upgrades for our brains long ago in the Bible. As Paul told the Romans:

*God knew what he was doing from the very beginning. He decided from the outset to shape the lives of those who love him along the same lines as the life of his Son.* (Romans 8:29)

God made our brain so he could shape us into the likeness of his own Son. What love! What brilliance! I am not surprised at this because God's entire creation showcases his brilliance every day. What surprises me is that humans still insist on being the center of attention. How can we rightly claim ownership of the potential power of our thoughts to improve our brain? I was once part of the zealous crowd that instructed everyone to replace their negative thoughts with positive ones in order to improve their own lives. I practiced this model for my first thirty years as a counselor. When I went to graduate school to become a Christian counselor, I discovered that Christian programs were using the same cognitive models of positive thinking to which the secular programs were devoted. Since that time, in my personal and professional continuing education of the Bible and the brain, God has showed me a huge insight that has been missing in the writing and speaking of the Christian counseling community.

---

| *Uplifting* | *Discouraging* |
|---|---|
| ➢ | ➢ |
| ➢ | ➢ |
| ➢ | ➢ |

## *Five Senses, One Focus*

What has been missing for the Christian counseling community? Until the advent of FocusChoice Therapy, we have not had our own therapy model to follow. We have worked off a hodgepodge of secular therapists' cognitive therapies and tried to integrate Biblical principles into these modalities. However, just like water won't mix with oil, Christian principles cannot effectively blend with secular therapy models. There is the fundamental difference that inhibits the merger of Christian beliefs with secular therapies. At the core of secular therapy is the belief that self-change is possible. FocusChoice Therapy and any future Christian models can only be grounded in God-change, not self-change. What is so remarkable for me is that God-change lines up perfectly with discoveries about how God made the brain.

For the Christian counselor, the centrality of the power of thoughts in transforming the brain is more important than humans transforming their own minds. Because our own thoughts have been cursed, the only transforming power of human thoughts is negative change. If you examine the current state of human misery, it confirms in my mind that human thinking destroys rather than heals. I possess such a strong feeling of new hope when I read about new brain discoveries that line up one hundred per cent with God's ageless teaching in the Bible. When we examine what the Bible says about the brain, we can clearly see how God intended his endless supply

| *Uplifting* | *Discouraging* |
|---|---|
| ➢ | ➢ |
| ➢ | ➢ |
| ➢ | ➢ |

of supernatural thoughts to be available to continually reinvent the brain he placed in each of us. God wants only his thoughts to program the brain cells. God's vast supply of uplifting thoughts surge into our brain cells when we focus on him with all of our five senses. The apostle Paul wrote to the Philippians about what happens when we focus on God so he can fill our minds with his thoughts:

> *Summing it all up, friends, I'd say you'll do best by filling your minds and meditating on things true, noble, reputable, authentic, compelling, gracious—the best, not the worst; the beautiful, not the ugly; things to praise, not things to curse.* (Philippians 4:8)

What an amazing transformation would occur throughout the entire world if every man and woman simply acknowledged God as the programmer of their brain. Seem impossible? God only asks each one of us to make the continual, conscious choice to be fully connected to him with our five senses. At the risk of sounding corny, God simply asks us to always be in his WiFi zone. The beauty of God's WiFi is that he offers free, unlimited universal coverage—there is absolutely no place where God has weak or no coverage. God provides perfect, clear reception everywhere. We simply must choose to show up with our sensory antennas directed to him.

---

| *Uplifting* | *Discouraging* |
|---|---|
| ➤ | ➤ |
| ➤ | ➤ |
| ➤ | ➤ |

## *Renewal at the Cellular Level*

What can we expect if we refuse to acknowledge God as our programmer and insist that we built our own brain? Remember, God made all brains the same. However, God's design only works properly when we acknowledge him as the programmer. Adam and Eve were the first to venture out and try to be self-programmers when they chose to eat the fruit from the tree of knowledge. As a result, we are all pre-programmed because of the curse we inherited from them. From infancy, we are naturally inclined to fill our brain cells with our own thoughts. And our own thoughts lean hard to the negative side because they are cursed.

In Debbie Hampton's article[1], "How Your Thoughts Change Your Brain, Cells and Genes," she states:

> So, if you have been bombarding your cells with peptides from negative thoughts, you are literally programming your cells to receive more of the same negative peptides in the future. What's even worse is that you're lessening the number of receptors of positive peptides on the cells, making yourself more inclined towards negativity.

In other words, our only self-programming ability is to make our curse worse. In my own life and the lives of the many clients I have counseled, I can attest that our own thinking has certainly resulted in more and more negativity over the years.

| *Uplifting* | *Discouraging* |
|---|---|
| ➤ | ➤ |
| ➤ | ➤ |
| ➤ | ➤ |

Secular therapists and many Christian therapists have habitually insisted that we can reprogram our own minds by switching our thoughts from negative to positive. How can we expect our own negative mind to flip to positive thinking? God's design of the brain does not allow us to pull off that reversal. In fact, when our negative mind tries to pull off a positive thought, it fails because it ends up reacting with more negativity. We would not need God if we could, in fact, do our own reprogramming. The good news is God designed the brain to be resilient when we trade in our pathetic thinking for his uplifting thoughts. Debbie Hampton continues:

> Every cell in your body is replaced about every two months. So, the good news is, you can reprogram your pessimistic cells to be more optimistic by adopting positive thinking practices...

God made our brains to regenerate so quickly, but he does not expect any of us to reprogram from pessimism to optimism on our own. Our repetitive failures to achieve this switch only produces additional pessimism. Taking the above quote a step farther, the actual good news for us is how quickly God designed the brain to respond once we choose to let God think for us. God produces change quickly when we flip from our thinking to his thoughts. I remember the days of re-hauling the tractor engines on our dairy farm. It was a time-consuming job. Fortunately, God's computerized engine in us—our brain—does not need to be re-hauled. Our dirty-thought fluids simply need to be replaced with his clean-living water.

---

| *Uplifting* | *Discouraging* |
|---|---|
| ➢ | ➢ |
| ➢ | ➢ |
| ➢ | ➢ |

## *Making the Right Choice*

To return to the last quote from Debbie Hampton's article[1], the author suggests "adopting positive thinking practices" as the way to "reprogram your pessimistic cells to be more optimistic." Of course, all of us would do that in a heartbeat if that suggestion actually worked. But it doesn't. What *does* work is simply letting God be our programmer. This is what God has wanted all along. God is the one who designed our brain so that "You are speaking to your genes with every thought you have"[1]. God set *himself* up, not us, to be the speaker. Human neuroscientists have labeled this process in the brain "epigenetics":

> You have a choice in determining what input your genes receive. The more positive the input, the more positive the output of your genes. Epigenetics is allowing lifestyle choices to be directly traced to the genetic level and is proving the mind-body connection irrefutable.[1]

I want to complete the puzzle when it comes to how God made the brain by adding that the God-mind-body connection is irrefutable. Yes, we do have a choice in determining what input our genes receive. However, the choice is not us inputting positive thoughts instead of negative ones. Brain research already shows that we cannot make positive thoughts magically appear out of a negative container. Only God can manufacture positive input. Our choice is to let God input his positive thoughts rather than us inputting our own

| *Uplifting* | *Discouraging* |
|---|---|
| ➤ | ➤ |
| ➤ | ➤ |
| ➤ | ➤ |

flawed (and therefore, negative) ones. We choose to allow God's thoughts for input by devoting the attention of our five senses to him.

The more consistently we choose God's thoughts for input, the more power we give him to sculpt our mind, body, and emotions into a Christ-like, caring, and loving human being.

> You have much more power than ever believed to influence your physical and mental abilities. Your mindset is recognized by your body—right down to the genetic level, and the more you improve your mental habits, the more beneficial response you'll get from your body. You cannot control what has happened in the past, which shaped the brain you have today, programmed your cells, and caused certain genes to switch on. However, you do have the power in this moment and going forward to choose your perspective and behavior, which will change your brain, cells, and genes. [1]

While this writing accurately describes how God made the brain to function, it does not describe how God can control this functioning. First, we don't have more power than ever believed. God has more power than we ever believed. Second, it is not us who improve our mental habits. Only God can make these improvements. How? Simply by giving him control of our mindset through keeping our five senses fixed on him. With God being able to program our mindset, he can—*and will*—take loving care of our mind and body right down to our

---

| *Uplifting* | *Discouraging* |
|---|---|
| ➢ | ➢ |
| ➢ | ➢ |
| ➢ | ➢ |

genes. Third, the author of this article says we can't control what has happened in the past. This is true. However, she then proclaims that we have the power in this moment and going forward to choose our perspective and behavior, which will change our brain, cells, and genes. This is not true! How is it possible that we could not have controlled what happened in the past, but now, magically, we have the power in this moment and in the future to choose our perspective and behavior? Unfortunately, this is well-intended anthropocentric hype without any substance. The only thing of substance is to live in this moment (and the future) with our five senses glued to God. This choice to focus on God comes directly out of our acknowledgement that we have no power outside of him. God has tons of power—supernatural power—to transform us, one moment at a time. With an infinite supply of thoughts to draw from, God never runs low on pouring out his thoughts on us to fuel positive change in us, from now until eternity.

| *Uplifting* | *Discouraging* |
|---|---|
| ➢ | ➢ |
| ➢ | ➢ |
| ➢ | ➢ |

|  Uplifting | Discouraging |
|---|---|
| ➢ | ➢ |
| ➢ | ➢ |
| ➢ | ➢ |

## *Faulty Thinking*

The truth is we never stopped pouring our own thoughts into our thinking vessel. In fact, one of the most common presenting problems that patients want to talk about in counseling is racing thoughts. Patients describe their thoughts as running in circles or running into dead ends. They also complain about not being able to turn their thoughts off or being stuck in their own thinking. Jeffrey M. Schwartz, M.D., a practicing neuropsychiatrist affiliated with UCLA, developed a four-step method to assist people in overcoming obsessive-compulsive behavior. His book, entitled *Brain Lock*,[3] describes the approach of cognitive self-therapy and behavior modification he believed would help people avoid "thinking traps." Dr. Schwartz even acknowledged that people have automatic tendencies toward faulty thinking, but describes how patients can use the mind to fix the brain. As with many other secular and even Christian counseling experts, he asserts that our human mind can be trained to "manually override" these automatic tendencies. Once again, this is where faulty thinking undermines humanistic theories. How can anyone overcome faulty thinking with a faulty-thinking hard drive. Only God can overcome our faulty thinking with his divine thinking. That is how God designed the brain.

Neuroscientists are not missing the point about how brilliantly God made the brain, including its neuroplasticity. But they are missing the most brilliant part of all. God is not asking us to do the impossible and repair the damaged hard

---

| *Uplifting* | *Discouraging* |
|---|---|
| ➢ | ➢ |
| ➢ | ➢ |
| ➢ | ➢ |

drive. Rather, God installs a super(natural) hard drive to replace our damaged one. His divine thinking replaces our entombed thinking. This is the big secret that was hidden from me by false teaching all these years. God does not want us to try to fix our own thinking. God wants to think for us. He can, and will, as we make the conscious, continuous choice to simply live in the moment with him through our sensory focus.

| *Uplifting* | *Discouraging* |
|---|---|
| ➤ | ➤ |
| ➤ | ➤ |
| ➤ | ➤ |

## *Through a New Lens*

Another word encountered frequently among counselors who are learning about how God made the brain is "mindfulness." Daniel J. Siegel, M.D., wrote a book called *Mindsight*[4] that provides tremendous clarity about the design of our brain and how it can function in a remarkable fashion:

> Mindsight acts as a very special lens that gives us the capacity to perceive the mind with greater clarity than ever before. This lens is something that virtually everyone can develop. ...[M]indsight allows us to examine closely, in great detail and depth, the process by which we think, feel, and behave. It also allows us to reshape and redirect our inner experiences so that we have more freedom of choice in our everyday actions....
>
> It helps us to be aware of our mental processes without being swept away by them, enables us to get ourselves off the autopilot of ingrained behaviors and habitual responses, and moves us beyond the reactive emotional loops we all have a tendency to get trapped in.

Like other secular brain specialists, Dr. Siegel runs into trouble with his theories. He rationalizes that we develop an amazing new lens using the faulty lens that created our dysfunctional ingrained behaviors and habitual responses in the past and up to the present. Any of us could easily understand that a lens crafter could not develop a great new

| *Uplifting* | *Discouraging* |
|---|---|
| ➢ | ➢ |
| ➢ | ➢ |
| ➢ | ➢ |

lens by starting with a defective lens. As I have written repeatedly, our own lens is cursed. Nothing we can ever do will make a faulty lens give us new, clear vision. Paul makes this connection crystal clear to the Ephesians:

> *Everything—and I do mean everything—connected with that old way of life has to go. It's rotten through and through. Get rid of it! And then take on an entirely new way of life—a God-fashioned life, a life renewed from the inside and working itself into your conduct as God accurately reproduces his character in you.* (Ephesians 4:22-24)

I am thrilled how these verses line up exactly with how God made our brain. Neuroscientists are absolutely correct concerning the details of their discoveries about the brain. They are simply missing the main point. It is not *our* mindsight, but God's mindsight that reshapes and redirects our inner experiences. God's mindsight gives us more freedom of choice in our everyday actions and more power for the future. Using his thoughts to transform our lives, God wears perfect lenses—he has 20/20 vision. God installs his lens in us to make us aware of our mental processes without being swept away by them. God's lens in us turns off the autopilot of our ingrained behaviors and habitual responses. This moves us beyond the reactive emotional loops we have been trapped in because of our own cursed lens.

---

| *Uplifting* | *Discouraging* |
|---|---|
| ➢ | ➢ |
| ➢ | ➢ |
| ➢ | ➢ |

## *Abnormally Positive Psychology*

Psychiatrists, psychologists, and counselors around the world are looking to apply advancements in neuroscience in their clinical practices and in university classrooms. Martin Seligman, Ph.D., a psychologist at the University of Pennsylvania, has been a leader in this endeavor. When I was in college, our class used his book *Abnormal Psychology*[5] as our textbook. Today, Dr. Seligman has shifted his focus to the other side of psychology. He is commonly known as the founder of Positive Psychology and has heavily promoted this therapy model since the year 2000. This is from the website of the Positive Psychology Center at the University of Pennsylvania (https://ppc.sas.upenn.edu/):

> *Positive Psychology* is the scientific study of the strengths that enable individuals and communities to thrive. The field is founded on the belief that people want to lead meaningful and fulfilling lives, to cultivate what is best within themselves, and to enhance their experiences of love, work, and play.

Although humans differentiate the scientific and the spiritual, God's design for the human brain clearly shows that he is the Master Scientist. The brain that God created is a spectacular invention that has taken mankind centuries to comprehend. The common thread among all the innovations in neuroscience is the pivotal role assigned to thoughts in the operating mechanics of brain functioning. When the brain

---

| *Uplifting* | *Discouraging* |
|---|---|
| ➢ | ➢ |
| ➢ | ➢ |
| ➢ | ➢ |

malfunctions, much of the problem can be traced back to faulty thinking. Now, neuroscientists are promoting the idea that the well-functioning brain can be traced back to correct thinking. The prominence of thoughts in how God designed the brain is no mystery from a Biblical standpoint. Right off the bat, in Genesis, God made it clear that Adam and Eve were welcome to enjoy everything in the Garden of Eden except the tree of knowledge. Very clearly, God was instructing Adam and Eve to leave the responsibility of thinking to God. In other words, God said that the only way everything was going to run smoothly in the entire operation of creation was for God to be the producer or the programmer—THE BIG BOSS. God made it very clear we should avoid thinking on our own. He made the brain to function properly only when he thought for us. Very simply put, God's thoughts produce a positive life; man's thoughts produce a negative life. Epigenetics, neuroplasticity, mindsight, and positive psychology only have true value when God's thoughts are the key to transformation.

| *Uplifting* | *Discouraging* |
|---|---|
| ➢ | ➢ |
| ➢ | ➢ |
| ➢ | ➢ |

# ...and the Pursuit of Happiness

Neuroscience experts, counseling experts, and Christian counseling experts all have a common ground for agreement: the brain is the control room for happiness or misery in life. Within that control room, everyone pretty much agrees that thoughts play a major role in determining a positive or negative outcome. Years ago, and even today, people have been instructed to change their thoughts from negative to positive. I do believe if people could do this on their own, we certainly would be living in a "wonderful world" by now. Yet, our world is more dangerous and has more evil people on the loose than ever before. In the 1960s and 70s we sang rock songs about living in "the eve of destruction." It seems our world is closer to mass destruction than ever before. With the new discoveries about the vast potential of our brain to be happy, exactly what is the problem?

The Greater Good Science Center started offering a free Science of Happiness online course in 2014 (http://greatergood.berkeley.edu/news_events/event/the_science_of_happiness). Since the course was launched, "...more than 375,000 students have registered for this course." This one indicator alone tells us that masses of people care about being happy. The course website's overview includes this:

> The free eight-week course explores the roots of a
> happy and meaningful life through science and practice.

| *Uplifting* | *Discouraging* |
|---|---|
| ➢ | ➢ |
| ➢ | ➢ |
| ➢ | ➢ |

Students will engage with some of the most provocative and practical lessons from the latest research, discovering how cutting-edge research can be applied to their own lives.

The Science of Happiness zeroes in on a fundamental finding from positive psychology: that happiness is inextricably linked to having strong social ties and contributing to something bigger than yourself—the greater good.

The Pursuit of Happiness web site lists "The 7 Habits of Happy People" (http://www.pursuit-of-happiness.org/):

1. Relationships
2. Acts of Kindness
3. Exercise and Physical Wellbeing
4. Flow
5. Spiritual Engagement and Meaning
6. Strengths and Virtues
7. Positive Mindset: Optimism, Mindfulness and Gratitude

Of all the areas studied in the relatively young field of positive psychology, gratitude has perhaps received the most attention. Grateful people have been shown to have greater positive emotion, a greater sense of belonging, and lower incidence of depression and stress.

| *Uplifting* | *Discouraging* |
|---|---|
| ➢ | ➢ |
| ➢ | ➢ |
| ➢ | ➢ |

I could not agree more with these observations. Quite frankly, "The Science of Happiness" sounds very familiar to my favorite science book of all: The Bible. I am not sure why this material is being presented as cutting edge and new. In the hippy culture in which I grew up, we had our own version of happiness. What is new is the scientific discovery of how God made the brain. What is fascinating about this discovery is the potential God gave the brain to be happy. My question to everyone (especially in the counseling profession) is: When are we finally going to turn to the Bible to get our answers for happiness?

| *Uplifting* | *Discouraging* |
|---|---|
| ➢ | ➢ |
| ➢ | ➢ |
| ➢ | ➢ |

| *Uplifting* | *Discouraging* |
|---|---|
| ➢ | ➢ |
| ➢ | ➢ |
| ➢ | ➢ |

## Something Bigger Than Yourself

The brain can manufacture happiness through thoughts that impact us down to the level of our genes. The Bible is also exact in the steps that lead to happiness. Unfortunately, the Bible has often been labeled as telling us the right way to live instead of the happy way to live. Even though the Bible is clear that living right comes from being happy, most people have missed that teaching. I missed that teaching until I learned how God made the brain. The Bible and the brain are in exact alignment with each other. As I explain how happiness precedes righteousness, please remember that both God—the Master Scientist—and human scientists use the same ingredients, with one critical, game-changing difference. God, the divine scientist, is the author and finisher of happiness and right living. Human scientists leave God out of the scientific equation. This one omission has totally screwed up mankind's ability to be happy and live right since the beginning of time.

So, why have we, the so-called followers of Christ, missed the boat when it comes to putting happiness before right living? One of my biggest excuses is I never knew how God made the brain. Another excuse is I was taught incorrectly. While it is true that the Old Testament featured right living, the New Testament did feature happy living. I confess that my desire to read the Bible was very low until I finally admitted that my life was unmanageable and I was powerless to be happy on my own. Once I learned God didn't design my brain

| *Uplifting* | *Discouraging* |
|---|---|
| ➤ | ➤ |
| ➤ | ➤ |
| ➤ | ➤ |

so I could be happy on my own, my desire to discover how God is the only way to happiness skyrocketed. And, being happy in God is the only way to right living.

I doubt most neuroscientists, after discovering how the brain and its thoughts are so tantamount to happiness, would acknowledge their discoveries lead us back to God. But I am eternally grateful that their discoveries have lead *me* back to God. My continual prayer is that learning how God made the brain will lead us all back to him. What is sweeter to me every day is God's brilliant architecture of finding closeness with him through the front door of the brain: our five senses. There is nothing more desirable than discovering sensory union with God; our brains closely attach with God so he can have free reign to run everything. What a simple, yet powerful, scientific invention on God's part! For me, the happiness begins at the beginning. God runs everything else in our brains and lives to ensure true happiness, regardless of whatever circumstances we may be enduring. The free course at Berkeley that teaches happiness is "inextricably linked to social ties and contributing to something bigger than yourself— the greater good" could not be more accurate. This truth can also be observed in Alcoholics Anonymous and the many other self-help programs. For me, it is even more easily observed in God's design for our happiness. God is the ultimate definition of something bigger than yourself. God is also the ultimate in close sensory attachment and emotional-social connection.

---

| *Uplifting* | *Discouraging* |
|---|---|
| ➢ | ➢ |
| ➢ | ➢ |
| ➢ | ➢ |

## *God Has a Plan*

God made our brains to have an entry point where we can closely attach to him through our five senses, thereby inviting him to be our 24/7, day-by-day producer and programmer for a lifetime of happiness. God also makes sure he surrounds us with his breathtaking presence. Simply by looking at snow-covered Rocky Mountain peaks in Colorado, I feel close to God. Not only does God surround me with his beauty, God's beauty lives in me. With every breath I take and every heartbeat I feel, God reminds me that he lives in me as well as surrounds me. I hope you can imagine what I felt like when I learned that God lives in my brain, *and* he wants to run my brain and my whole life with his thoughts. I can certainly imagine how you will feel when you embrace this certainty.

I admit that not all that long ago, I still believed the lie that church leaders taught me—that God only spoke to people during Biblical times. Of course, I didn't know he spoke to me until I learned that God made my brain so I could closely relate to him through my five senses. Now I hear God talk to me with his thoughts all day long. His constant communion with me makes me feel so loved and happy that I long to never interrupt his thoughts with my own. Giving God the full focus of my five senses and constantly hearing his voice is my one true source of happiness. For so many years my own thoughts made me unhappy, and now I understand why. Learning that the

| *Uplifting* | *Discouraging* |
|---|---|
| ➢ | ➢ |
| ➢ | ➢ |
| ➢ | ➢ |

thoughts we have affect us, right down to every cell in our body, has had a profound and lasting effect on my life. This explained exactly why my life had been so miserable for so many years. I was consumed with my own thinking. Now, I am blissfully happy because God's thoughts consume me. I marvel at God's direction for my life. He is starting and completing work in and through me that I could have never imagined. For God to use me to be the founder of the first genuine Christian counseling model and tell me that FocusChoice Therapy will impact the world for his Kingdom's sake goes far beyond my natural human desires. Especially at my advanced maturity (i.e., age), I did not dream of world outreach. Fortunately, God has not sent me on some wild goose chase. God is bringing everything together as I marvel at his hard work. I simply want to follow wherever he leads me.

| *Uplifting* | *Discouraging* |
|---|---|
| ➢ | ➢ |
| ➢ | ➢ |
| ➢ | ➢ |

## *The Happy Quitter*

Exactly how did God design the brain so he could fill me with such desire that makes me happy and ensures that I live right? I was certainly not able to live right on my own thinking. My own thinking made me miserable. In my misery, I had no desire to do what was right. My only desire was to escape. Little did I know that God offers us the great escape, a heavenly escape to which no earthly escape can compare. I learned about this heavenly escape when I learned about how God made the brain. In his unbelievable wisdom, God offers us an escape to him at the entry point of our five senses. Yes, giving our senses of sight, sound, smell, taste, and touch to God is escaping to him. Escaping to God with our five senses sets our brain in motion, in God's motion. Putting our senses on him puts our mind at rest. Our own thoughts stop, while God's thoughts spring into action. His thoughts make us feel good instead of bad, they inspire us instead of defeat us, they show love instead of hate, they do good instead of evil. You may be asking, "Do God's thoughts in us make us do good?" They certainly do! Re-read about how God made the brain. God programmed our brain to perform at the sound of his voice. But, we can only hear God's voice when ours is quiet, and our voice is quiet only when we are attentive to God with our five senses. This is what God will do when we have our sensory focus on him:

| *Uplifting* | *Discouraging* |
|---|---|
| ➢ | ➢ |
| ➢ | ➢ |
| ➢ | ➢ |

*We use our powerful God-tools for smashing warped philosophies, tearing down barriers against the truth of God, fitting every loose thought and emotion and impulse into the structure of life shaped by Christ. Our tools are ready at hand for clearing the ground of every obstruction and building lives of obedience into maturity.* (2 Corinthians 10:5-6)

Just reading these words gives me a rush of inspiration to keep my five senses firmly glued to God. Seeing in words what God will do in and through us takes on a whole new meaning for me now that I have learned how God made the brain. What is most inspiring is that my only part is paying attention to God with my five senses. That is something I can do without mental effort (and something we all can do without human performance). Not that I am lazy. If anything, I already work too hard. I simply got so sick and tired of trying to do good and live right on my own horsepower that I finally gave up and quit. Yes, I am a quitter. A happy quitter! Quitting on myself and begging God to take over the reins of my life at the ripe old age of sixty now stands out as a landmark decision in my life. O HAPPY DAY!!!!!

| *Uplifting* | *Discouraging* |
|---|---|
| ➤ | ➤ |
| ➤ | ➤ |
| ➤ | ➤ |

## *Spreading the Good News*

Wait a minute. Here I am, a Christian counselor developing the first actual God-based therapy model using the Bible and the brain as my primary sources of information. And I am teaching people to be happy quitters?! After almost forty years of seeing clients and their families for counseling, I have thousands of examples of people who are ecstatic to be given permission to quit trying to change on their own. They are tired of trying and trying and trying only to hear some counselor tell them to try even harder. People who make an appointment to see me know I am a Christian counselor, and they are eager to hear my approach for change. They are highly receptive to hear that my instruction will be based on what the Bible says and how God made the brain, and that I will teach them how to let God change them.

Every client admits they have never heard instruction from the Bible that is taught within the context of how God made the brain. I am not the least bit surprised by their admission. I was never taught, either. In fact, our church leaders and Christian counselors have not been taught about the insight from the Bible on how God made the brain. At every level of secular and Christian education, teachers have failed to teach students how their brain works. For many years, the lack of instruction was because neuroscience was just developing. Yet, even now, when neuroscience is making so

| *Uplifting* | *Discouraging* |
|---|---|
| ➢ | ➢ |
| ➢ | ➢ |
| ➢ | ➢ |

many fascinating discoveries about how God made the brain, Christian leaders and counselors are lagging in their learning. I am so inspired by what God has been teaching me about the Bible and the brain. I will share this learning through every possible venue and with everyone, everywhere around the world, who will listen.

| *Uplifting* | *Discouraging* |
|---|---|
| ➢ | ➢ |
| ➢ | ➢ |
| ➢ | ➢ |

## Our Failure at Self-change

So, here is the million-dollar question: Why are so many people who come to me for counseling so ready to quit? After hearing the stories of pain and misery that people experience, and listening to their frustration in trying to fix life problems on their own, I am not surprised they have reached the end of their rope. I hear stories many times over from married couples who can't stand to have dinner together, let alone sleep together. When I listen to how they talk to each other in my office, their disgust with their partner is beyond belief. Although they claim they want to stop hating their spouse, they seem helpless to stop talking their ugly talk. These couples would even try their best to use new dialogues with each other that I tried to teach them. We would practice and practice together. They would try their best at home to use these new dialogues, but would end up feeling like failures.

Many clients who would come to me for individual counseling experienced the same frustrations as couples. What they said to themselves was so ugly. Their self-talk was deplorable. They felt such hate for themselves. Like with couples, I would teach them new self-dialogues and we would practice in the office. But as much as they would try at home to change their internal script, the result was the same as with the couples. These individuals would end up feeling like failures, and their negative self-talk got even worse.

---

| *Uplifting* | *Discouraging* |
|---|---|
| ➢ | ➢ |
| ➢ | ➢ |
| ➢ | ➢ |

These failures made me question myself. Was something wrong with these individuals and couples? Was something wrong with me? Was I a bad counselor? To be sure, I felt like a bad counselor. My self-talk was very negative, too. What was my problem? As a counselor and a Christian I should have known better. Right?

After all, I went through graduate school in secular counseling and I went to another graduate school twenty years later for Christian counseling. I honestly admit I was not devoted to studying the Bible. And, just like everyone else, I sure had no clue how God made the brain. My re-training starting with learning about how God made the brain. Neurons in the brain handle sensory input from our five senses (and all the nerve endings in our skin). Neural pathways help create patterns in how we think and act. When we choose to give God the attention of our five senses, he ends up determining the way we think, learn, move, and behave.

As I learned how he made the brain, God made me eager to read the Bible through his lens rather than my own. Yes, reading about how God made the brain taught me why I could not change and why I could not change my clients. I learned that God did not even design the brain to be capable of self-change. God created the brain so that it only worked properly with him as the signal caller. Plus, God said anyone and everyone can make him their Lord simply by choosing to focus on God with their five senses. That is why I quit on myself. I am so happy I did!

---

| *Uplifting* | *Discouraging* |
|---|---|
| ➢ | ➢ |
| ➢ | ➢ |
| ➢ | ➢ |

## *No Help Needed*

So, let's apply the scriptures to everything I've written so far. Believe me, I want nothing to do with writing a book that has anything to do with self-change. I want every word to reflect God's teaching, not my own. I simply want to be the messenger. So, let's start with what God says about self-change. Since therapy is all about change, this seems like a good starting point to me. Let's get right down to business. One thing we have all heard in church at one point or another is that we cannot free ourselves from sin. What does the Bible say about self-change when it comes to sin? Here is how Paul explained it to early Christians in Ephesus:

> *It wasn't so long ago that you were mired in that old stagnant life of sin. You let the world, which doesn't know the first thing about living, tell you how to live. You filled your lungs with polluted unbelief, and then exhaled disobedience. We all did it, all of us doing what we felt like doing, when we felt like doing it, all of us in the same boat. It's a wonder God didn't lose his temper and do away with the whole lot of us. Instead, immense in mercy and with an incredible love, he embraced us. He took our sin-dead lives and made us alive in Christ. He did all this on his own, with no help from us! Then he picked us up and set us down in highest heaven in company with Jesus, our Messiah.* (Ephesians 2:1-6)

| *Uplifting* | *Discouraging* |
|---|---|
| ➢ | ➢ |
| ➢ | ➢ |
| ➢ | ➢ |

This scripture is loaded with truth that tells exactly what the Bible says about sin and self-change. What stands out to me is that sin is not just about one bad action. Sin is about our whole life and our ethos, and applies to every one of us. We have all been mired in sin and unable to change ourselves. In fact, we stagnated so badly in our sin that we were dead. We could not bring ourselves back to life. God could have easily written us off, but in his mercy and love, God single-handedly brought us back to life—with absolutely no help from us. Even better, he did not just barely restore us back to life, God elevated us to a life on the same level as his own Son, Jesus. These verses clearly show me that only God can set me free from sin. Only God can change me, and no amount of help from me is necessary or beneficial.

| *Uplifting* | *Discouraging* |
|---|---|
| ➤ | ➤ |
| ➤ | ➤ |
| ➤ | ➤ |

## Keep Your Eyes on Jesus

Here is another million-dollar question: If I am not capable of self-change, and only God can change me, then what is my role? Of course, by now, you know that I am going to say that my only role is to give God my total sensory focus. That is the only way I will notice what God is thinking, saying and doing to change my life. What does the Bible say?

> *Do you see what this means—all these pioneers who blazed the way, all these veterans cheering us on? It means we'd better get on with it. Strip down, start running—and never quit! No extra spiritual fat, no parasitic sins. Keep your eyes on Jesus, who both began and finished this race we're in. Study how he did it. Because he never lost sight of where he was headed—that exhilarating finish in and with God—he could put up with anything along the way: Cross, shame, whatever. And now he's there, in the place of honor, right alongside God. When you find yourselves flagging in your faith, go over that story again, item by item, that long litany of hostility he plowed through. That will shoot adrenaline into your souls.* (Hebrews 12:1-3)

These verses clearly validate the role of sensory focus. Keep your eyes on Jesus and never quit. The verses go so far as to instruct us to shed off anything that distracts from our attention being on God. They also show us how to keep the

| *Uplifting* | *Discouraging* |
|---|---|
| ➤ | ➤ |
| ➤ | ➤ |
| ➤ | ➤ |

adrenaline pumping to prevent us from getting discouraged. As part of sensory focus on God, visualize the saints cheering us on. In fact, right now, visualizing my dad encouraging me to keep writing gives me goose bumps. My sensory memory takes me back to Friday night football games when I would hear his voice cheering while I was on the field playing the game. These verses also tell us to keep our eyes on Jesus by being steadfast in our study of how he ran the race. If we ever get off track by thinking about ourselves, remembering the hardships Jesus endured will get our attention off ourselves and back on Jesus. This scripture is really powerful to me in light of what I have learned about how God made the brain. I want to keep my focus on God so I am not distracted by my own cursed, negative thoughts. With my thoughts held captive, God's thoughts reign in my mind and change my whole being, right down to my genes.

| *Uplifting* | *Discouraging* |
|---|---|
| ➢ | ➢ |
| ➢ | ➢ |
| ➢ | ➢ |

## *God's Truth Permeates All*

How does God change me right down to my genes? Researching this "how" part in the Bible and in brain studies has been a fascinating journey. The way in which the Bible and the brain line up is outright uncanny. I may be in my sixties, but God has filled me with a new passion I have never felt before to comprehend how much the Bible and the brain are in sync. For example:

> *God's wisdom is something mysterious that goes deep into the interior of his purposes. You don't find it lying around on the surface. It's not the latest message, but more like the oldest—what God determined as the way to bring out his best in us, long before we ever arrived on the scene. (1 Corinthians 2:7-9)*

When you pair this scripture with recent brain research and put the two side by side, the true genius of God is revealed. In her article, Debbie Hampton[1] wrote:

> Thoughts sculpt your brain...[W]hen people consciously practice gratitude, they get a surge of rewarding neurotransmitters, like dopamine, and experience a general alerting and brightening of the mind, probably correlated with more of the neurochemical norepinephrine.

---

| *Uplifting* | *Discouraging* |
|---|---|
| ➢ | ➢ |
| ➢ | ➢ |
| ➢ | ➢ |

Talk about a direct connection between the Bible and the brain! God made our brain so his thoughts can bring out the best in us and brighten our minds and bodies down to a cellular level. God's wisdom is not just a surface-level experience; his thoughts go deep into our bones. God's truth permeates the core of our very being. When we give God the complete focus of our five senses, we open access to the very depths of our heart. God made our brain this way so the anchor of his love would penetrate throughout our mind and body much deeper than any pain or hurt anchored from our past. God is the only anchor upon which we can always depend. God is our only hope, especially when we are feeling stuck in our pain.

*Bend an ear, God; answer me.*
   *I'm one miserable wretch!*
*Keep me safe—haven't I lived a good life?*
   *Help your servant—I'm depending on you!*
*You're my God; have mercy on me.*
   *I count on you from morning to night.*
*Give your servant a happy life;*
   *I put myself in your hands!*
*You're well-known as good and forgiving,*
   *bighearted to all who ask for help.*
*Pay attention, God, to my prayer;*
   *bend down and listen to my cry for help.*
*Every time I'm in trouble I call on you,*
   *confident that you'll answer.* (Psalm 86:1-7)

---

    *Uplifting*                                        *Discouraging*

➤                                  ➤

➤                                  ➤

➤                                  ➤

These uplifting verses are anchor thoughts for me. I can always rely on these promises from God when I feel my worst and am in my deepest pain. I used to think I would be perpetually stuck in my pain. However, thanks to these verses and others and knowing how God made my brain, I am assured of him giving me a happy life. My absolute confidence is in every uplifting thought God offers me. This is exactly how God sculpts my brain. His thoughts literally cause a chain reaction of neurochemical changes in my body. They give me a dopamine surge of divine magnitude.

| *Uplifting* | *Discouraging* |
|---|---|
| ➤ | ➤ |
| ➤ | ➤ |
| ➤ | ➤ |

|  Uplifting  |  Discouraging  |
|---|---|
| ➢ | ➢ |
| ➢ | ➢ |
| ➢ | ➢ |

# God is Creator of Life and Happiness

It doesn't surprise me that counseling professionals are seeking therapy models that promote happiness. The world in which we live has become overrun with hurt and pain. With the brain discoveries of how thoughts are instrumental to changing our whole being, it also does not surprise me that counseling professionals are highlighting positive thinking more than ever before. Unquestionably, all the brain studies feature the profound positive impact that uplifting thoughts can have in our lives. And lastly, I am not surprised that God is not receiving credit for being the originator of the thoughts that make us happy. After all, credit was taken away from God and given to evolution as the author of designing the earth and every living thing that occupies this place. Just look to what extremes negative human thinking tries to take us. Human thinking has taken us to such negative extremes that God has been discredited for creating life and making happiness. Despite the deplorable condition that our whole world is in right now, mankind still chooses to follow its own thinking rather than God. Believe me, my life had deteriorated into such a deplorable condition that I was elated to learn that God designed my brain in such a way that he can run my life and make me happy. This learning finally turned on the light as to what God has been wanting to show me through the Bible all these years.

---

*Uplifting* *Discouraging*

➢ ➢

➢ ➢

➢ ➢

God wanted to show me (and everyone else) the same truth he tried to show Adam and Eve at the beginning of time. God made Adam and Eve to live in sensory time with him in the plush and beautiful of Garden of Eden while God did all the thinking on their behalf. God made the brain with a sensory side for Adam and Eve to enjoy being happy with God. He made a thinking side to be occupied by his perfect divine thoughts. That way God could be the programmer for all of mankind. God would then have man and woman multiply his entire creation with people and his love. Instead, Adam and Eve chose to delve into God's cognitive domain when they pursued the tree of knowledge. Eating that first fruit began centuries of stinkin' thinkin' through which mankind has polluted the world with its own cursed thoughts. Man's thoughts can only bring sadness and hate into the world. Only God's thoughts can bring happiness and love into the world. That's how God designed the brain to function in the first place. God didn't create the human brain for mankind to produce happiness through their own thinking.

---

| *Uplifting* | *Discouraging* |
|---|---|
| ➤ | ➤ |
| ➤ | ➤ |
| ➤ | ➤ |

## *God's House of Thoughts*

With neuroscientists discovering that thoughts in the brain are closely linked to happiness, the only step left is to connect how God made the brain and what the Bible says about happiness. The Bible is very clear about the connection between thoughts and happiness. There are many scriptures throughout God's Word about this connection. The Psalms contain many prayers of David that support this connection. David describes how he made the connection between thankful thoughts and happiness in Psalm 9:1-2:

*I'm thanking you, GOD, from a full heart,*
  *I'm writing the book on your wonders.*
*I'm whistling, laughing, and jumping for joy;*
  *I'm singing your song, High God.*

In Psalm 35:9-10, David describes how happy he is:

*But let me run loose and free,*
  *celebrating GOD'S great work,*
*Every bone in my body laughing, singing, "GOD,*
  *there's no one like you.*
*You put the down-and-out on their feet*
  *and protect the unprotected from bullies!"*

---

| *Uplifting* | *Discouraging* |
|---|---|
| ➢ | ➢ |
| ➢ | ➢ |
| ➢ | ➢ |

This Psalm (63:6-8) describes David as being happy even when he can't sleep:

*If I'm sleepless at midnight,*
  *I spend the hours in grateful reflection.*
*Because you've always stood up for me,*
  *I'm free to run and play.*
*I hold on to you for dear life,*
  *and you hold me steady as a post.*

David says he would rather live in God's House of Thoughts than at a beautiful resort (Psalm 84:10-11):

*One day spent in your house, this beautiful place of worship,*
  *beats thousands spent on Greek island beaches.*
*I'd rather scrub floors in the house of my God*
  *than be honored as a guest in the palace of sin.*

In his letter to the Philippians, Paul wrote about being very happy. Ironically, many of his letters and other writings were written when he was in jail, but his spirit never dampened. In perhaps his happiest letter, Paul describes how he was feeling to the Christians of Philippi:

*I'm glad in God, far happier than you would ever guess—happy that you're again showing such strong concern for me. Not that you ever quit praying and*

| Uplifting | Discouraging |
|---|---|
| ➤ | ➤ |
| ➤ | ➤ |
| ➤ | ➤ |

*thinking about me. You just had no chance to show it. Actually, I don't have a sense of needing anything personally. I've learned by now to be quite content whatever my circumstances. I'm just as happy with little as with much, with much as with little. I've found the recipe for being happy whether full or hungry, hands full or hands empty. Whatever I have, wherever I am, I can make it through anything in the One who makes me who I am.* (Philippians 4:10-13)

| Uplifting | Discouraging |
|---|---|
| ➢ | ➢ |
| ➢ | ➢ |
| ➢ | ➢ |

| *Uplifting* | *Discouraging* |
|---|---|
| ➤ | ➤ |
| ➤ | ➤ |
| ➤ | ➤ |

## Fill Your Mind with the Best

When reading about men like David in the Old Testament or Paul in the New Testament, it is very clear to me that happiness is more closely connected to a person's thoughts rather than their circumstances. Given that, what does the Bible say about how thoughts determine happiness? In his letter to the Philippians, Paul is very clear on this subject:

*Summing it all up, friends, I'd say you'll do best by filling your minds and meditating on things true, noble, reputable, authentic, compelling, gracious—the best, not the worst; the beautiful, not the ugly; things to praise, not things to curse. Put into practice what you learned from me, what you heard and saw and realized. Do that, and God, who makes everything work together, will work you into his most excellent harmonies.* (Philippians 4:8-9)

The last part of this scripture says unmistakably that God makes us happy. The first part of this scripture tells us to fill our minds with positive thoughts instead of negative ones. That brings us to another "how" question. How do we fill our minds with uplifting thoughts rather than downcast thoughts? The secular Positive Psychology theorists would argue that mankind does the work of replacing our negative thoughts with positive ones we produce and use to fill our mind. My FocusChoice Therapy model strongly opposes that secular

| *Uplifting* | *Discouraging* |
|---|---|
| ➢ | ➢ |
| ➢ | ➢ |
| ➢ | ➢ |

view based on what this scripture says. This scripture does not say that we use our own thoughts to fill our mind with positivity. After all, that would contradict other scriptures in the Bible that clearly indicate we should not think for ourselves and try to live life on our own efforts. Paul's letter to the citizens of a busy and powerful Rome certainly challenged their thinking:

> *Those who think they can do it on their own end up obsessed with measuring their own moral muscle but never get around to exercising it in real life. Those who trust God's action in them find that God's Spirit is in them—living and breathing God! Obsession with self in these matters is a dead end...* (Romans 8:5-6)

I really like how this scripture points out that our own thinking results in a dead end. To me, that is very consistent with the theme of the whole Bible, beginning in the Garden of Eden when Adam and Eve ate the fruit from the tree of knowledge and cursed human thoughts forever. Whose thinking do we fill our mind with instead of our own? Going back to Philippians 4:8-9, Paul tells us to fill our minds with what we saw and heard and learned from him. What did Paul teach? Look again at Romans 8:5-6 where Paul says that we can trust God's action in us to the point that we find out that God's Spirit lives and breathes God in us. In other words, when we put our sensory focus on God, we learn that he fills our minds so much with uplifting thoughts that we literally breathe God.

---

| *Uplifting* | *Discouraging* |
|---|---|
| ➢ | ➢ |
| ➢ | ➢ |
| ➢ | ➢ |

## High on God

When we live and breathe God's thoughts, what can we expect? Just how high (in a good way) can God's uplifting thoughts take us? Let's label this process in the brain as a supernatural high. After all, God did create our bodies to release pleasure chemicals. We can clearly say God wants us to get high. His thoughts will lift us higher than any other "high." One of my favorite scriptures that lifts me higher every time I read it is Isaiah 43:2-4:

*I've called your name. You're mine. ...*
*I paid a huge price for you: ...*
*That's how much you mean to me!*
*That's how much I love you!*

Here's another favorite scripture that helps me to relax and not feel pressure to perform:

*God can do anything, you know—far more than you could ever imagine or guess or request in your wildest dreams! He does it not by pushing us around but by working within us, his Spirit deeply and gently within us.* (Ephesians 3:20)

These verses from Psalm 61:3-4 also help me to relax and calm down:

| Uplifting | Discouraging |
|---|---|
| ➢ | ➢ |
| ➢ | ➢ |
| ➢ | ➢ |

*You've always given me breathing room,*
*   a place to get away from it all,*
*A lifetime pass to your safe-house,*
*   an open invitation as your guest.*

What is so encouraging to me is that God has given me a lifetime invitation to escape to the safety of his arms through sensory focus. God made my brain to be able to focus on him to escape the pressures of life by simply being in the moment with him through my five senses. God surrounds me with his presence through creation and lives inside me through his Spirit. My only part is to tap into this presence with my eyes, ears, nose, mouth and hands. God made all of us this way so we everyone has an open invitation to escape to God!

This next scripture reminds me how often I desire to run to the Lord:

*"Are you tired? Worn out?... Come to me...Walk with me and work with me—watch how I do it... Keep company with me and you'll learn to live freely and lightly."* (Matthew 11:28-30)

Once again, God gives us an open invitation to spend sensory time with him. When we do, he will teach us how to live in happiness. Rather than being stuck in our own thoughts which make us tired and worn out, we can allow God's thoughts to make us happy. What a difference to escape to God!

---

| *Uplifting* | *Discouraging* |
|---|---|
| ➢ | ➢ |
| ➢ | ➢ |
| ➢ | ➢ |

## Great Sensory Escapes

Many of my clients and readers feel helpless when it comes to obsessive thinking. They are unable to stop their repetitive and racing thoughts. Any attempts to figure out or reason with these thoughts only causes more obsession. Our culture has erroneously tried to teach us that we can think our way out of anything. However, our brains are simply not designed to think our way out of obsessive thoughts. Our brain is designed rather brilliantly to switch to the sensory side and escape these obsessive thoughts.

A young male client of mine with Asperger's Syndrome was especially prone to hyper-focus on obsessive thoughts. Remember the doomsday prediction that the world would end in December 2012? My client fixated on that prediction for more than a month as that date neared. He could not sleep, he lost his appetite, he could not concentrate on his school work. In addition, he could not stop himself from sharing his obsessive thoughts with classmates, who belittled him. He was convinced I could not help him stop his thoughts even for a single minute. I assured him I could stop his thoughts for at least five minutes if he agreed to play the Magic Piano app on my iPhone. This app required the sensory attention of his fingers, his ears, and his eyes. With the focus of these three senses, his brain was thought-free. He learned in a few minutes how sensory focus can suppress obsessive thinking.

| *Uplifting* | *Discouraging* |
|---|---|
| ➤ | ➤ |
| ➤ | ➤ |
| ➤ | ➤ |

The more senses we include in our escape to God, the more likely the sensory side of our brain will be able to override and silence our thinking brain. As successful as this simple approach is, most people feel very uncomfortable applying this technique on a regular basis. We feel out of character simply because we are not accustomed to feeling in the sensory moment. Maybe on vacation, maybe during exercise, maybe watching or attending a sporting event. Probably during sex where we can engage all five of our senses. But how about at work? Or when we first wake up in the morning? I used to be so stuck in the thinking side of my brain that I would wake up realizing I had fallen asleep the night before from being exhausted from overthinking. I would think about work while brushing my teeth, shampooing my hair, even eating my breakfast. My overthinking was so out of hand that I would forget if I had shampooed my hair. Or forgot to rinse off. Yea, life was tough.

Then I started to focus on the rhythmic sensations of brushing my teeth, and the aromas while shampooing my hair. Focusing on the sensations of these morning tasks quieted my overthinking mind. Now, I live my life in the sensory moment all day long. Hmm. Do I never think? I now live in freedom, with thoughts coming to me rather than me searching for them. I have been so happy living in sensory time. Allowing thoughts to come to me naturally, rather than experiencing the frustration of trying to search for them, is an ongoing wonderful daily experience.

---

| *Uplifting* | *Discouraging* |
|---|---|
| ➢ | ➢ |
| ➢ | ➢ |
| ➢ | ➢ |

## *Nowhere Else to Turn*

I have learned over the many years of both my personal and professional life that most of us only become willing to be in continual prayer with God when we have nowhere else to turn. For me, it has taken quite a few nowhere-else-to-turn experiences before I became ready and willing to keep following God on an ongoing basis through sensory devotion. However, I would always look away from God once my crisis appeared to be over and I was feeling better again. I would go back to reliance on my own thinking to run my life, despite God's promise in Psalm 91:14-16:

> *"If you'll hold on to me for dear life," says* GOD,
>   *"I'll get you out of any trouble.*
> *I'll give you the best of care*
>   *if you'll only get to know and trust me.*
> *Call me and I'll answer, be at your side in bad times;*
>   *I'll rescue you, then throw you a party.*
> *I'll give you a long life,*
>   *give you a long drink of salvation!"*

This scripture is very clear about holding onto God for dear life to get us out of any trouble. Considering we live in a violent world and terrible trouble can hit us at any time, we would all be wise to hang onto God at all times. Since hanging onto God simply means keeping our five senses glued to him,

| *Uplifting* | *Discouraging* |
|---|---|
| ➢ | ➢ |
| ➢ | ➢ |
| ➢ | ➢ |

we are all capable of sensory devotion without trying. We simply choose to be in sensory addiction to God rather than earthly gods. Please don't wait until you are 60 years old like I was before you start hanging onto God through continual prayer.

None us know when a big crisis might hit and we feel like we're at the end of our rope once again. We live in an angry society because of mankind's wicked thoughts. Psalm 119:25-32 is one of my favorite scriptures to focus on God when I feel down and out:

> *I'm feeling terrible—I couldn't feel worse!*
>    *Get me on my feet again. You promised, remember?*
> *When I told my story, you responded;*
>    *train me well in your deep wisdom.*
> *Help me understand these things inside and out*
>    *so I can ponder your miracle-wonders.*
> *My sad life's dilapidated, a falling-down barn;*
>    *build me up again by your Word.*
> *Barricade the road that goes Nowhere;*
>    *grace me with your clear revelation.*
> *I choose the true road to Somewhere,*
>    *I post your road signs at every curve and corner.*
> *I grasp and cling to whatever you tell me;*
>    *GOD, don't let me down!*
> *I'll run the course you lay out for me*
>    *if you'll just show me how.*

| *Uplifting* | *Discouraging* |
|---|---|
| ➢ | ➢ |
| ➢ | ➢ |
| ➢ | ➢ |

The words "dilapidated, a falling-down barn" jumped out at me because I grew up in a dairy farm area in Pennsylvania. I would see those poor barns every day. They never got any attention. No one cared about their worn-out condition. My thoughts are like one of those run-down barns. My thoughts don't care about me. They only give me negative attention. They only make me feel more run down and worn out. I wondered how I make the "old barn" of myself new once more.

| Uplifting | Discouraging |
|---|---|
| ➤ | ➤ |
| ➤ | ➤ |
| ➤ | ➤ |

| Uplifting | Discouraging |
|---|---|
| ➢ | ➢ |
| ➢ | ➢ |
| ➢ | ➢ |

## *Old Barns Made New*

There are scripture verses that spell out how our own thoughts make us feel worn out and run down, such as in Paul's letter to the Galatians:

> *It is obvious what kind of life develops out of trying to get your own way all the time: repetitive, loveless, cheap sex; a stinking accumulation of mental and emotional garbage; frenzied and joyless grabs for happiness; trinket gods; magic-show religion; paranoid loneliness; cutthroat competition; all-consuming-yet-never-satisfied wants; a brutal temper; an impotence to love or be loved; divided homes and divided lives; small-minded and lopsided pursuits; the vicious habit of depersonalizing everyone into a rival; uncontrolled and uncontrollable addictions; ugly parodies of community. I could go on.* (Galatians 5:19-21)

It wears me out just to read about all the ugliness that results from focusing on our own thinking. No wonder our world is such a mess. So many people rely on their own thinking and are so determined to get their own way. Nothing good comes out of trying to think for ourselves and run our own lives. Our own thoughts cannot make us happy. They are too screwed up. It is impossible to get happy thoughts out of such awful thinking. We claim we want to run our own lives to be free. But the guaranteed outcome is becoming a slave to a

| *Uplifting* | *Discouraging* |
|---|---|
| ➢ | ➢ |
| ➢ | ➢ |
| ➢ | ➢ |

joyless, loveless, paranoid, angry, emotionally impotent, small-minded, depersonalized, uncontrollable, addicted, ugly daily life. Not one ounce of happiness will come out of our own thoughts.

By simply making a continual, conscious choice to pay full attention to God with our five senses, God will wash away our terrible thoughts by flooding us with his happy thoughts. The next verses in Galatians give an exhilarating description of what God's thoughts can do for us:

> *But what happens when we live God's way? He brings gifts into our lives, much the same way that fruit appears in an orchard—things like affection for others, exuberance about life, serenity. We develop a willingness to stick with things, a sense of compassion in the heart, and a conviction that a basic holiness permeates things and people. We find ourselves involved in loyal commitments, not needing to force our way in life, able to marshal and direct our energies wisely.* (Galatians 5:22-23)

What a happy life is possible simply by giving our sensory attention to God so he can flood our minds with his thoughts! At the age of 64, I am experiencing God's supernatural happiness despite becoming a senior citizen. Please start to experience God's joy regardless of your age, young or old. Clients of every age—children, teens and adults—come to me broken down and worn out. Our pitiful old barn can be made brand new, regardless of who we are.

---

| *Uplifting* | *Discouraging* |
|---|---|
| ➢ | ➢ |
| ➢ | ➢ |
| ➢ | ➢ |

## *Trust*

How does God lay out a course for me to follow so I can run free? God thinks for me and speaks for me. God even behaves for me. God takes over my actions throughout the day. God shows me how to live each moment of every day. My only part is to live in sensory communion with him. How is this possible? We live in a culture and church atmosphere where individualism, independence and personal performance are expected and exhibited more than ever before. How unpopular to suggest that we invite God to think, talk and behave on our behalf. We are simply to focus and follow. The Bible makes it clear that this is the only path to freedom and happiness. God simply wants us to rest and relax in him while he dwells in us and lives his life in and through us. God literally wants to carry us on his back. God's Word spells out this plan and purpose for each of us:

> *Listen to me, family of Jacob, everyone that's left of the family of Israel. I've been carrying you on my back from the day you were born, and I'll keep on carrying you...when you're old and gray. I've done it and will keep on doing it, carrying you on my back, saving you.* (Isaiah 46:3-4)

How do we allow God to carry us on his back? There is only one way. That is to keep our five senses glued to him. If you have ever allowed anyone to carry you on their back,

| *Uplifting* | *Discouraging* |
|---|---|
| ➤ | ➤ |
| ➤ | ➤ |
| ➤ | ➤ |

you discover the meaning of dependency. You discover the meaning of trust. Trust is not about a feeling of confidence. It is about holding on for dear life, even though you might be terrified. Your arms wrap tightly around the neck of the person who is carrying you. Your legs wrap tightly around their waist. You experience every move they make. You can hear them breathe and see where they are taking you. I lived in Virginia Beach when my girls were young, and would take them to the beach. When we went into the ocean they would hang onto me you dear life as I would ride up over a wave and down again. God instructs us to trust him with all of our five senses:

> *Trust God from the bottom of your heart; don't try to figure out everything on your own. Listen for God's voice in everything you do, everywhere you go; he's the one who will keep you on track. Don't assume that you know it all. Run to God! Run from evil! Your body will glow with health, your very bones will vibrate with life!* (Proverbs 3:5-8)

---

| *Uplifting* | *Discouraging* |
|---|---|
| ➤ | ➤ |
| ➤ | ➤ |
| ➤ | ➤ |

## *Faith, Hope, and Trust*

God carries us on his back when we give God the full attention of our five senses and live in sensory communion with him. This is the definition of where he leads me, I will follow. Sensory focus on God is the essence of faith, hope and trust in God. Faith, hope and trust are not intended to be feeling words. They are action words about choosing to direct our sight, smell, sound, taste, and touch to God. They are action words about choosing to partake in the fact that we are already in God's presence. God surrounds us with his creation and his Spirit lives in us. We partake by living in the moment with God using one or more of our senses to experience his beauty around us or feel his love in us. This sensory experience with God silences our own negative, cursed thoughts. God then fills the thought cavity of our brain with his uplifting thoughts. This is the only way to live a free and abundant life.

As my readers and clients give me feedback on starting to live in the freedom of a FocusChoice life, one of their most frequent concerns is: "If I am feeling angry or anxious, does that mean I am not free? Does that mean I should feel ashamed and guilty because I am not letting God carry me?" Absolutely not! Just like my little girls feeling scared and holding onto me for dear life as we encountered the ocean waves at Virginia Beach, the same is true as we choose to have God carry us through the waves of life. Feeling scared or angry does not mean we have abandoned our dependency on God. Psalms, the

| *Uplifting* | *Discouraging* |
|---|---|
| ➢ | ➢ |
| ➢ | ➢ |
| ➢ | ➢ |

longest book in the Bible, has chapter after chapter of David being afraid and angry. Yet, God described David as a man after his own heart.:

> *'I've searched the land and found this David, son of Jesse. He's a man whose heart beats to my heart, a man who will do what I tell him.'* (Acts 13:22)

Our heart beats with God's heart when we are in constant sensory communication with him. Being anxious or angry does not mean we are apart from God. God created us, including our feelings of anxiety and anger. God simply wants us to share our feelings of anger and anxiety with him, which is precisely what David did throughout the book of Psalms. Reading the Psalms is a great way to discover how to share our feelings with God.

Paul tells the Ephesians that feeling angry is not a reason to feel ashamed or guilty before God. Growing up in a culture and church atmosphere that condemns us for feeling anger and anxiety—our own stinkin' thinkin'—is what has caused our shame and guilt, not God:

> *Go ahead and be angry. You do well to be angry—but don't use your anger as fuel for revenge. And don't stay angry. Don't go to bed angry. Don't give the Devil that kind of foothold in your life. (Ephesians 4:26-27)*

Basically, God is letting us know all our feelings are a fundamental and necessary part of our sensory relationship

---

| *Uplifting* | *Discouraging* |
|---|---|
| ➢ | ➢ |
| ➢ | ➢ |
| ➢ | ➢ |

with him. Paul is telling the Ephesians—and us—that God is welcoming us to share our anger with him. God especially wants us to share our anger with him before we sleep at night. When Paul wrote to the Philippians, he told them God advises us to share our worry or anxiety with him:

> *Don't fret or worry. Instead of worrying, pray. Let petitions and praises shape your worries into prayers, letting God know your concerns. Before you know it, a sense of God's wholeness, everything coming together for good, will come and settle you down. It's wonderful what happens when Christ displaces worry at the center of your life.* (Philippians 4:6-7)

I have always been able to worry without even trying. It comes naturally to me. When I tried to stop worrying, I ended up being more worried. Now, I have accepted that my own thoughts will never overcome worry. Since I have chosen to place my sensory focus on God, he has displaced worry at the center of my life. The thoughts that God pours into my life are free of worry.

| *Uplifting* | *Discouraging* |
|---|---|
| ➤ | ➤ |
| ➤ | ➤ |
| ➤ | ➤ |

| *Uplifting* | *Discouraging* |
|---|---|
| ➤ | ➤ |
| ➤ | ➤ |
| ➤ | ➤ |

## *A New Normal*

At first, many of my clients struggle with the teaching of freedom in Christ through a continual sensory attachment to God. Like I have always been in my life, they are so attached to their own thinking that it feels very unnatural to dwell in sensory time with God and not be thinking for themselves. Yet, to think for ourselves requires a huge effort and causes lots of stress. We are so accustomed to this inner tension in our mind and body that it feels natural in an almost comforting way. It is our "normal." Yes, I am saying that feeling free in Christ does not feel normal, at least not at the beginning of our transition to a FocusChoice life. Our own sinful tendency is to make sensory focus a struggle by critiquing this experience with our own flawed thinking.

Now, here comes the tricky part. As I share this observation with clients struggling with sensory focus, they condemn themselves and even fear I am judging them or scolding them. Not at all! I am quick to encourage and tell them of course we all are very prone to slip back into our own thinking mode. We have done it our entire lives. It takes time and practice to experience the feeling of freedom now that we have been taught how to live in freedom. When they catch themselves slipping back into their own thinking, I tell clients to accept this as normal. Then use the slip as a reminder to switch back into sensory mode.

| *Uplifting* | *Discouraging* |
|---|---|
| ➤ | ➤ |
| ➤ | ➤ |
| ➤ | ➤ |

I spend a lot of time in therapy sessions reminding my clients of their own successful moments of living in sensory time. Recently, a young client shared his fear of regressing back into effort-based, stressed-out living as he pondered his future, including where to live and what career to choose. He began to guilt himself for still living with his parents. I thanked him for sharing his fear with me and encouraged him to share these feelings with God as they entered his mind. Then I reminded him how good he felt at our previous session. He had shared with me his experience of sensory freedom riding his bike on the country roads where he lived. He remembered God talking to him while he rode. God had shared his thoughts with my client about his strong interest in a graphic design career and gave my client the idea to put together a portfolio. God even made some great suggestions on what to include in his portfolio. I then read a Bible verse to my client where God promises to complete the work in us that he started:

> *There has never been the slightest doubt in my mind that the God who started this great work in you would keep at it and bring it to a flourishing finish on the very day Christ Jesus appears.* (Philippians 1:6)

Just like this client, I remember feeling weak when I would turn to God in a crisis. I shamed myself for even feeling the need to run to God for help. I was supposed to be strong in myself so I could show God what a good Christian I was. As a result, when God would talk to me and show me what to do, I would go back to reliance on my own thinking to carry out

---

| *Uplifting* | *Discouraging* |
|---|---|
| ➤ | ➤ |
| ➤ | ➤ |
| ➤ | ➤ |

what God showed me. Not surprisingly, that is what I was taught my entire life in my culture and church. It was my job to complete what God gave me. I have now learned that I could no more carry out what God started in me than I could have rescued myself in the first place.

| *Uplifting* | *Discouraging* |
|---|---|
| ➤ | ➤ |
| ➤ | ➤ |
| ➤ | ➤ |

|  Uplifting  |  Discouraging  |
|---|---|
| ➢ | ➢ |
| ➢ | ➢ |
| ➢ | ➢ |

## *Living in Rhythm with God*

Trying to complete on my own what God began in me reminds me of a statement a client made to me a few years ago. He believed that we are saved by grace, but it is our job to work out our salvation. Here's what Paul had to say about this matter:

> *What I'm getting at, friends, is that you should simply keep on doing what you've done from the beginning. When I was living among you, you lived in responsive obedience. Now that I'm separated from you, keep it up. Better yet, redouble your efforts. Be energetic in your life of salvation, reverent and sensitive before God. That energy is God's energy, an energy deep within you, God himself willing and working at what will give him the most pleasure.* (Philippians 2:12-13)

We work out our salvation the same way God saved us, by his grace. Our "work" does not consist of our human mental effort to perform, but our ongoing choice to keep our sensory attention on God. In fact, these verses encourage us to redouble this "responsive obedience" or sensory obedience. Responsive is a sensory word. God wants our obedience to him to start with keeping our five senses glued to him. Then God wants us to "redouble" or heighten our focus on him with our eyes, ears, nose, mouth, and hands. The example I use for myself is when I listen to music. I can be somewhat attentive

| *Uplifting* | *Discouraging* |
|---|---|
| ➢ | ➢ |
| ➢ | ➢ |
| ➢ | ➢ |

to the sound of the drums; or, I can tune in very closely and really get into their rhythm. God desires that we tune in our senses to him at a very intense level, which ensures that our stinkin' thinkin' shuts down. We are so tuned into God at that point that our own thoughts shut down. God created our brain to function this way.

Our sensory attachment to God ensures that we live in rhythm with him. This is the only way possible to follow God and live in obedience to him with our words and actions. What we focus on with our five senses determines how we speak and behave. The phrase "sensitive before God" is the outcome of this sensory fine tuning. This level of sensory focus makes us feel so alive. When we obey God at this level with our five senses we become energetic in our life of salvation. God supplies this energy as he pours out his thoughts and words. He becomes our energy source and our power as he works in and through us. We simply focus and follow. God lives deep in us and captures this energy to do what gives him the most pleasure. God makes me feel so important to him. God wants to utilize me, which gives him pleasure. God's pleasure is to save all of us. He is not willing to allow any of us to perish. He wants all of us to have eternal life:

> *He is restraining himself on account of you, holding back the End because he doesn't want anyone lost. He's giving everyone space and time to change.* (2 Peter 3:9)

---

| *Uplifting* | *Discouraging* |
|---|---|
| ➢ | ➢ |
| ➢ | ➢ |
| ➢ | ➢ |

## *To Rest Is To Work*

God loves us like no one else can. His strongest desire is that we all get saved so we can experience life with him in this world and in heaven. God knows that to ensure our salvation he must do all the work from start to finish. That's how much God loves us. He knows we always mess up his work when we infiltrate our own thoughts into his domain. That is why God instructed Adam and Eve to stay away from the tree of stinkin' thinkin' in the first place. He loved them and wanted them to be content in the beautiful Garden of Eden. He knew they would destroy their happiness and hurt themselves by partaking of the tree of knowledge. God spells out this necessity of himself doing all the work for us in scripture:

> *Now God has us where he wants us, with all the time in this world and the next to shower grace and kindness upon us in Christ Jesus. Saving is all his idea, and all his work. All we do is trust him enough to let him do it. It's God's gift from start to finish! We don't play the major role. If we did, we'd probably go around bragging that we'd done the whole thing! No, we neither make nor save ourselves. God does both the making and saving. He creates each of us by Christ Jesus to join him in the work he does, the good work he has gotten ready for us to do, work we had better be doing.* (Ephesians 2:7-10)

| *Uplifting* | *Discouraging* |
|---|---|
| ➤ | ➤ |
| ➤ | ➤ |
| ➤ | ➤ |

When I read this scripture for the first time, it appeared to contradict itself. It says God does all the work and for a good reason. If it was our work, we'd just go around bragging about our accomplishments (which is true; our culture and church constantly give high praise to the self-made man or woman). But, at the end of these verses, it tells us to join God in the work he does and adds this is the work we should already be doing. God quickly showed me there is no contradiction in this scripture. These verses simply say that our work is to do God's work. As the scripture spells out, our work is to trust God enough to let him do all the work. Our work in this context is very different than the definition of work put on us by our culture and church. They define work as using our brain to figure out life on our own and then to putting our mental effort into action to follow through with our behaviors. I lived the first 60 years of my life trying to be self-responsible. I failed miserably. I understand where this scripture says God wants me to be. God has me right where he wants me when I trust him with my sensory focus. The result is I rest in God with my five senses while he showers his grace and kindness upon me. Can this possibly be true? My work is to rest in him?

---

*Uplifting* *Discouraging*

➤  ➤

➤  ➤

➤  ➤

## *Rest in God's Garden*

My work is to rest in him? This was such a foreign concept to me. How is that even possible? Reading the Bible and learning how God made the brain fully explains how it is not only possible but how it is the only path to happiness. To borrow the phrase from the school at Berkeley, this is God's "Science of Happiness." God designed our brain so we live in the moment with him using our five senses, giving him our full attention while he walks with us and talks with us. God directs each word we share and every move we make. While we are fully focused on God with the sensory side of our brain, God occupies the thinking side of our brain. This ensures that we follow him in our words and actions all day long. God's framework is for us to relax in him with our five senses while he does all the work in our lives. This is the only path to true happiness. The words of the famous hymn "In the Garden," written by C. Austin Miles in 1912, still ring true today:

> I come to the garden alone,
> While the dew is still on the roses;
> And the voice I hear, falling on my ear,
> The Son of God discloses.
>
>> And He walks with me, and He talks with me,
>> And He tells me I am His own,
>> And the joy we share as we tarry there,
>> None other has ever known.

*Uplifting*                                   *Discouraging*

➢                                              ➢

➢                                              ➢

➢                                              ➢

He speaks, and the sound of His voice,
Is so sweet the birds hush their singing,
And the melody that He gave to me,
Within my heart is ringing.

    God's desire is that we dwell in his garden, from the start of each day while the morning dew still moistens his creation, and all day long. God created our brain to be able to experience his garden by living in the moment with our senses fully alert to him. God wants our sensory receptors to experience his sounds, his colors, his fragrance, his touch and even his flavors. The only thing that can dull our senses is being distracted by our own thoughts. Unlike cell phone or WiFi providers, there are no dead spots or poor reception with God. On his end, God always stays in close sensory connection with us. If we remain steadfast in resisting our natural urge to think with our own thoughts, God will continue connection by using our brain as a container for his thoughts. Our close sensory connection with God will ensure we never miss God's call.

---

| *Uplifting* | *Discouraging* |
|---|---|
| ➤ | ➤ |
| ➤ | ➤ |
| ➤ | ➤ |

## *A Circle of Angels*

With the incredible way God designed our brain—to continually hear his voice through dwelling in close sensory attachment to him—I can embrace the many scriptures in the Bible that describe resting in God no matter what our circumstances. The twenty-third Psalm is my favorite example:

*Even when the way goes through*
  *Death Valley,*
*I'm not afraid*
  *when you walk at my side.*
*Your trusty shepherd's crook*
  *makes me feel secure.*

*You serve me a six-course dinner*
  *right in front of my enemies.*
*You revive my drooping head;*
  *my cup brims with blessing.*

*Your beauty and love chase after me*
  *every day of my life.*
*I'm back home in the house of* GOD
  *for the rest of my life.* (Psalm 23:4-6)

Such an amazing scripture! God always walks by our side; but, we can only feel his presence when we abide in him

| *Uplifting* | *Discouraging* |
|---|---|
| ➤ | ➤ |
| ➤ | ➤ |
| ➤ | ➤ |

with our five senses. When we attach to God's voice, and his sounds, sights, smells, and touch, we cannot miss God's presence by our side. He surrounds us from every direction. In fact, as these verses say, God's beauty and love chase us every day of our lives. We don't have to go anywhere to search for him. We simply switch from the thinking side of our brain to the sensory side. God made this switch a simple choice, and it yields immediate results. We will never have to wait for God to be close to us when we use one or more of our senses in a rhythmic fashion to experience his presence in and around us.

Another of my favorite scriptures in Psalms describes our resting in God and being free from our anxious fears:

*God met me more than halfway. He freed me from my anxious fears.*

*Look at him; give him your warmest smile.*
*Never hide your feelings from him.*

*When I was desperate, I called out,*
*and God got me out of a tight spot.*

*God's angel sets up a circle,*
*of protection around us while we pray.*

*Open your mouth and taste, open your eyes and see—how good God is.*
*Blessed are you who run to him.* (Psalm 34:4-8)

By running to God, these verses do not mean that we have to search for him. God is already in our presence and has

| *Uplifting* | *Discouraging* |
|---|---|
| ➢ | ➢ |
| ➢ | ➢ |
| ➢ | ➢ |

his senses glued to us. He just wants us to meet him halfway by gluing our senses to him. We are to look at God with our eyes and smile at him with our mouth. He wants us to open our mouth and taste, and open our eyes and see—how good God is. When we remain in prayer through continually giving him the attention of our five senses, God has his angels set up a circle of protection around us. That is the only way to feel safe so we can rest.

| *Uplifting* | *Discouraging* |
|---|---|
| ➢ | ➢ |
| ➢ | ➢ |
| ➢ | ➢ |

| Uplifting | Discouraging |
|---|---|
| ➤ | ➤ |
| ➤ | ➤ |
| ➤ | ➤ |

# Getting into the Zone

> *Are you tired? Worn out? Burned out on religion? Come to me. Get away with me and you'll recover your life. I'll show you how to take a real rest. Walk with me and work with me—watch how I do it. Learn the unforced rhythms of grace. I won't lay anything heavy or ill-fitting on you. Keep company with me and you'll learn to live freely and lightly.* (Matthew 11:28-30)

These could be the central theme verses for a sensory relationship with God. Are we tired and worn out from the burden of our own thinking? Our thoughts are too heavy and complicated to try to figure out. Our thoughts stress us out. They make us anxious. They cause us confusion. They make us feel angry and depressed. Of course they do! God never intended mankind to use the brain he gave us to do our own thinking. God wants to use our brain for his purposes. That is why he designed our brain so we could focus on him with our five senses. God uses the thinking side of our brain as a container for his thoughts. That is the only way he can run our lives. That is the only way we can rest in him while he works in us.

What does it look like to walk with him and work with him? Growing up as an athlete, one of my favorite descriptions is in Paul's first letter to the Corinthians, in which Paul uses the athlete to explain what our part looks like:

| *Uplifting* | *Discouraging* |
|---|---|
| ➢ | ➢ |
| ➢ | ➢ |
| ➢ | ➢ |

> *You've all been to the stadium and seen the athletes race. Everyone runs; one wins. Run to win. All good athletes train hard. They do it for a gold medal that tarnishes and fades. You're after one that's gold eternally.*
>
> *I don't know about you, but I'm running hard for the finish line. I'm giving it everything I've got. No sloppy living for me! I'm staying alert and in top condition. I'm not going to get caught napping, telling everyone else all about it and then missing out myself.* (1 Cor. 9:24-27)

At first, I was confused by these verses because training hard and running hard is a lot of effort. And yet, other verses say God does all the work, while we rest in him. How can we possibly reconcile these words that sound so contradictory? I didn't know this as a young athlete, but my recent learning about how God made the brain has taught me that the work of an athlete is about repetitive sensory training to heighten and fine-tune our focus. Sensory training for our muscles, and our visual and tactile focus. These verses prescribe sensory training so we stay alert—no sloppy living or getting caught napping. Renowned athletes are great because they have intense focus, not because they think intensely. In fact, their sensory focus is so intense that they are not thinking about anything. The best athletes get into "the zone"—*a sensory focus zone*—at the most critical moments in the game. The quarterback throws every pass perfectly. The receiver makes every catch because his eyes are so focused on the ball that he has no doubtful thoughts about catching it. The

---

| *Uplifting* | *Discouraging* |
|---|---|
| ➤ | ➤ |
| ➤ | ➤ |
| ➤ | ➤ |

best basketball players make every shot in the deciding fourth quarter. They are in such an intense sensory zone that their brain has no room to think or worry about messing up or losing the game. By putting your sensory focus on God, you, too, can get into the zone.

| *Uplifting* | *Discouraging* |
|---|---|
| ➤ | ➤ |
| ➤ | ➤ |
| ➤ | ➤ |

| Uplifting | Discouraging |
|---|---|
| ➢ | ➢ |
| ➢ | ➢ |
| ➢ | ➢ |

## *Use Your Passion*

In other words, our hard work is not mental work, but sensory work. We can all choose intense sensory focus, and there is always a level playing field. Although some people are said to be better thinkers than others, God says that our own thoughts are messed up. It doesn't matter if some people are perceived as more intelligent than others. God says we all need to be saved and rescued from our own cursed thinking.

In a sensory way, God has gifted each of us equally. He makes no distinction between us. God made us all equally capable to make the simple choice to devote our sensory focus to him. We all may have different passions which God gave us as a free gift. He simply desires that we use these sensory passions in a wholeness way that demonstrate God's love in us:

> *If you preach, just preach God's Message, nothing else; if you help, just help, don't take over; if you teach, stick to your teaching; if you give encouraging guidance, be careful that you don't get bossy; if you're put in charge, don't manipulate; if you're called to give aid to people in distress, keep your eyes open and be quick to respond; if you work with the disadvantaged, don't let yourself get irritated with them or depressed by them. Keep a smile on your face. (Romans 12:6-8)*

| *Uplifting* | *Discouraging* |
|---|---|
| ➢ | ➢ |
| ➢ | ➢ |
| ➢ | ➢ |

Paul shares very clear instructions from God in these verses. There is one and only one way to carry out these instructions: keep your five senses glued to God and follow his orders. Sensory attention to God is the only way our own thoughts are silenced enough to hear God's instructions. Otherwise, we will follow our own cursed thoughts, which preach our own message instead of God's Message. Our own thoughts will not help, but rather will absolutely take over. They will teach our junk, not God's divine wisdom. We will get bossy. We will manipulate. We will get irritated and depressed. For 60 years of my life I could not keep a smile on my face because I lived following my own thoughts. Now, I am old and grumpy and smile all day long. I am continually learning how to focus and follow, not adding my own thoughts, which is what made me tired and depressed. I simply teach what the Bible says and how God made our brain.

| Uplifting | Discouraging |
|---|---|
| ➢ | ➢ |
| ➢ | ➢ |
| ➢ | ➢ |

## *Embrace Every Moment in God*

How do I manage to live what I teach? Simply put, I could not manage my way out of a wet paper bag. But, God has clearly shown me how to live each moment of every day. How am I so certain of this? Because what the Bible says and how God made the brain are in perfect alignment. Paul tells the Romans—and me—exactly how to do this:

> *So here's what I want you to do, God helping you: Take your everyday, ordinary life—your sleeping, eating, going-to-work, and walking-around life—and place it before God as an offering. Embracing what God does for you is the best thing you can do for him. ...[F]ix your attention on God. ...Unlike the culture around you, always dragging you down to its level of immaturity, God brings the best out of you, develops well-formed maturity in you.* (Romans 12:1-2)

The words in these verses are very poetic, but how do we translate them into brain language? Sleeping, eating, driving, and walking are all sensory words. These are activities where God desires the focus of our five senses as an offering to him. "Embracing" is also a sensory term. We cannot embrace anything with our thoughts. We can embrace everything with our sight, sound, smell, taste, and touch. That is what it means to fix our attention on God, and the only way to embrace everything he does for us. In other words, give a

| *Uplifting* | *Discouraging* |
|---|---|
| ➤ | ➤ |
| ➤ | ➤ |
| ➤ | ➤ |

hearty welcome to God and his presence in us and around us. By fixing our five senses on him, we will not have our attention fixed on the culture around us. Focusing our senses on the culture around us drags us down to its level of immaturity. By looking to God with our senses, he carries us up to his level of maturity and brings out the best in us. Our culture drags us down to thinking it's cursed thoughts. God pulls us up to thinking his thoughts.

| *Uplifting* | *Discouraging* |
|---|---|
| ➤ | ➤ |
| ➤ | ➤ |
| ➤ | ➤ |

## *Become a Slave and Be Set Free*

The only way I manage to live a FocusChoice life is to offer my ordinary daily routine, and every moment of my day, to God for his use to carry out his plan to save the world. God wants me on his team! Yes, he wants all of us who are sick and tired of living our life for our own purposes. The bonus is that by offering ourselves through our sensory focus to him, God will lift the heavy burden of running our own life off our back. He will lift the heavy burden of doing our own thinking and the tiredness it brings. Simply by resting in God with our five senses, he gives us a loving and happy life while he carries out his work in and through us. Only God could pull off such a brilliant design for our brain! God can give us a free life through being a slave to him. It is the only kind of slave I ever want to be. A slave where the Master treats me a thousand times better than I treat myself. Not a slave where the master beats me down further than I already beat down myself.

A client recently shared his concerns with me about this plan. To give himself and his daily life as an offering to God meant that he would have to give up—sacrifice—his own desires. When I asked him for an example of sacrificing his own desires, he responded, "To give up doing what I want to do." When I asked him what he wanted to do, he said, "To have fun and enjoy life." I pointed out this is exactly what God promises to give us when we offer him our sensory focus. That

| *Uplifting* | *Discouraging* |
|---|---|
| ➢ | ➢ |
| ➢ | ➢ |
| ➢ | ➢ |

is precisely how God designed the brain to operate. That is precisely what God says over and over in the Bible.

The underlying problem with this client, and indeed many of us, is that we confuse our desires and our thoughts. No one has shown us that desires and thoughts are not mixed together in the same section of the brain. As a result, we lose track of what we desire versus what we think. This client was thinking that offering God his daily routines was giving up his desires. Not true! It is giving up our thoughts. It is giving up our control. Our cursed thoughts tell us we can only protect our desires and be happy by controlling our life by thinking for ourselves. The way God designed the brain is in opposition to what we think. God says that our desire to be happy and to feel loved and cared-for can only happen when we give up trying to control our own daily routines. We can only live freely by allowing God to think for us and let him tell us what to do. We put God in a position to think for us when we let go of our fixation on the routine itself. When we focus on the rhythmic sensations of the moment, we can focus on the thoughts God puts into our brain. We simply focus and follow.

---

*Uplifting*                    *Discouraging*

➢                              ➢

➢                              ➢

➢                              ➢

## *Sitting at God's Feet*

Brian Johnson of the Bethany Church wrote the following (original source unknown):

> All fear, hate, depression, anger, addiction, or whatever your issue is that's real in your life will bow in submission to God when you commit yourself to a continued posture of sitting at His feet. There isn't a person or quick fix that can or should take the place of that connect with Him. It is the reason Jesus was able to sleep through the storm. It is the reason why Jesus said "forgive them they don't know what they are doing" when He was hung on the cross. It's the reason He didn't turn the stone into bread in the desert when He was tested. People try and become God and take control of life but inside are never at peace. Peace with God is coming to grips with the fact that He is God and we are not and in turn acting like it.

I really like what Brian Johnson says in this passage. His writing is quite poetic, but may need some explanation. Let's translate this through the lens of how God designed the brain. From a brain perspective, it is not the mental decision to commit ourselves that matters. Our thoughts are defective and our mental commitments are useless. In fact, our mental promises trick us into believing that we have our own mental strength upon which we can rely to produce follow-through

| *Uplifting* | *Discouraging* |
|---|---|
| ➢ | ➢ |
| ➢ | ➢ |
| ➢ | ➢ |

with obedient behaviors. We can try to obey God with all the mental effort in the world yet we will fail every time. Even Paul admitted to the Romans that he could not trust his own thoughts to make himself obey:

> ... *'I know that all God's commands are spiritual, but I'm not. Isn't this also your experience?' Yes. I'm full of myself—after all, I've spent a long time in sin's prison. What I don't understand about myself is that I decide one way, but then I act another, doing things I absolutely despise. So if I can't be trusted to figure out what is best for myself and then do it, it becomes obvious that God's command is necessary.* (Romans 7:14-16)

It is the continual sensory practice of sitting at his feet that matters. Sitting at God's feet is how we bow in submission to God. Obedience to God occurs at the point of entry to our brain. When we are presented with incoming stimuli, it is the practice of submitting to God what we see, smell, hear, taste and touch that defines our obedience. This practice of sensory attention to God is not only the poetic definition of sitting at his feet, but also the practical definition. We sit at God's feet when we look into his loving eyes and feel him holding us so close we can hear him whisper into our ears. Our sensory devotion to God silences our thoughts so we can hear and live by what God tells us to think, what to say, and how to behave. The practice of "focus and follow" is what makes us happy instead of being angry, anxious, or depressed. We live in a

---

| *Uplifting* | *Discouraging* |
|---|---|
| ➢ | ➢ |
| ➢ | ➢ |
| ➢ | ➢ |

heavenly addiction to the heavenly God rather than a human addiction to one or more of many earthly gods. We are no longer addicted to the biggest (and most destructive) god, which is our own thinking. We become addicted to God's divine thoughts in us through the continual, conscious choice to give him the focus of our five senses. We obey whatever we are addicted to. I am happy to confess I have a heavenly addiction to God and his thoughts.

| *Uplifting* | *Discouraging* |
|---|---|
| ➢ | ➢ |
| ➢ | ➢ |
| ➢ | ➢ |

| Uplifting | Discouraging |
|---|---|
| ➢ | ➢ |
| ➢ | ➢ |
| ➢ | ➢ |

## *Understanding and Embracing Fear*

I want to explain (from the perspective of how God made the human brain) the role of fear in our lives. Brian Johnson[6] lumped the word "fear" with words like hate, depression, and addiction. Fear should not be grouped with these other words, which are the outcome of living in fear. We live in fear when we depend on our own thinking. This has been a reality since the time Adam and Eve chose to follow their own thinking instead of following God's thinking through sensory focus on him in the lush Garden of Eden.

Fear itself is important in our lives. God created the sensory cue of fear as an alarm signal to alert us when we are in either physical or emotional danger. God created our brain to seek refuge in him when we are afraid. He did not intend that we rush to our own thinking, which only produces more fear and more danger. Fear is our constant reminder to remain in close sensory attachment to God each minute of every day in our lives. With our sensory focus on God, we don't feel the fear because we are focused on him. We only live in fear when we live in our own thoughts. Our own thoughts are automatically fearful because they are defective and cursed. Our only release from fearful living is abandoning our own thoughts through sensory focus on God. I continually thank God for designing my brain to be afraid of my own thoughts. At the same time, I thank God for giving me refuge from my fears by sitting at his feet in sensory communion with him.

| *Uplifting* | *Discouraging* |
|---|---|
| ➢ | ➢ |
| ➢ | ➢ |
| ➢ | ➢ |

In "Reading the Bible"[6], Billy Graham wrote: "The Bible is not an option, it is a necessity." When I learned five years ago about how God made the brain, I discovered why reading the Bible was a necessity in my life. This discovery was not instant, but occurred over the course of three or four months. Nor did it come out of some mental commitment on my part. I simply began a sensory approach to reading God's Word after learning that God designed the sensory side of our brain to draw us to him. This sensory approach was quite simplistic. I did not put pressure on myself to achieve a goal of reading the Bible every day or even a goal of reading a certain number of verses in one sitting. I merely read to enjoy. Switching my approach from "I ought to read" to "I want to read" made all the difference in the world for me. As I engaged my senses as I read, my own thoughts were silenced. I became immersed in God's thoughts. By reading his Words written on the pages in the Bible, I began to hear God's voice show me what these words meant. God expounded and explained. His interpretations gave me insight beyond what I could ever imagine. His revelations gave me so much joy that I began to read every chance I could. God made me feel so special to him. Over time, reading the Bible became a longing, an addiction. This heavenly addiction became the springboard for writing books in which I could share with others what God was showing me. Reading and writing became my "go to" favorite way to remain in close sensory communion with God. It took me away from my own thoughts. It took me away from living in fear.

---

| *Uplifting* | *Discouraging* |
|---|---|
| ➢ | ➢ |
| ➢ | ➢ |
| ➢ | ➢ |

## *The Joy of the Lord is My Strength*

As I reflect on my personal experience of falling in love with God, I want to share scriptures about my transformation from living in the negativity of self-thinking to living in the joy of the Lord. This remarkable journey took me away from a lifetime of living in fear to a daily walk of happiness. There is a hymn I memorized in summer Bible school as a child, "The Joy of the Lord," written by Alliene Vale in 1971, is based on Nehemiah 8:10:

The joy of the Lord is my strength,
The joy of the Lord is my strength,
The joy of the Lord is my strength,
The joy of the Lord is my strength.

He heals the broken hearted and they cry no more,
He heals the broken hearted and they cry no more,
He heals the broken hearted and they cry no more,
The joy of the Lord is my strength.

He gives me living water and I thirst no more,
He gives me living water and I thirst no more,
He gives me living water and I thirst no more,
The joy of the Lord is my strength.

| *Uplifting* | *Discouraging* |
|---|---|
| ➢ | ➢ |
| ➢ | ➢ |
| ➢ | ➢ |

Here is another scripture that describes this transformation:

*And then take on an entirely new way of life—a God-fashioned life, a life renewed from the inside and working itself into your conduct as God accurately reproduces his character in you.* (Ephesians 4:24)

God reproduces his character in us when we simply follow the instructions he gives us:

*Watch what God does, and then you do it, like children who learn proper behavior from their parents. Mostly what God does is love you. Keep company with him and learn a life of love. Observe how Christ loved us. His love was not cautious but extravagant. He didn't love in order to get something from us but to give everything of himself to us. Love like that.* (Ephesians 5:1-2)

---

| *Uplifting* | *Discouraging* |
|---|---|
| ➢ | ➢ |
| ➢ | ➢ |
| ➢ | ➢ |

## *Our Thoughts are Crazy!*

The prophet Ezekiel explains how God changes us from the inside to love like him:

> *I'll pour pure water over you and scrub you clean. I'll give you a new heart, put a new spirit in you. I'll remove the stone heart from your body and replace it with a heart that's God-willed, not self-willed. I'll put my Spirit in you and make it possible for you to do what I tell you and live by my commands.* (Ezekiel 36:25-27)

Once again we read how the Bible is in exact alignment with the way God designed our brain. God made our brain for him to fill our thinking cavity with his thoughts while we focus on him on the sensory side of our brain. We are not capable of being God-willed when we think for ourselves. Only when God thinks for us are we able to do what he tells us and live by his commands. The first thing God tells us in the Ephesians verses is to "watch" him. We watch him by keeping continual "company" with him through sensory attention. We watch him, not only with our eyes, but also with our nose, our ears, our hands, and our mouth. Every one of our five senses is involved when we truly keep company with someone. I have a client who is blind. She cannot see me with her eyes, but she can "see" me so well with her other senses, which are extra alert as a result of her blindness.

| *Uplifting* | *Discouraging* |
|---|---|
| ➢ | ➢ |
| ➢ | ➢ |
| ➢ | ➢ |

Sensory attachment to God is the secret for him to be able to put his Spirit in us. Otherwise, we are filled with our own stone-cold spirit that contains our cursed thoughts, our cursed words, and cursed behaviors. We follow what we focus on. When we focus on our own thoughts, we follow our own thoughts with our words and actions. When we focus on God's thoughts through sensory attachment to him, our words and actions follow his thoughts. Plain and simple.

Paul put it in plain and simple language to the Galatians:

> *You crazy Galatians! Did someone put a hex on you? Have you taken leave of your senses? Something crazy has happened, for it's obvious that you no longer have the crucified Jesus in clear focus in your lives. His sacrifice on the cross was certainly set before you clearly enough. Let me put this question to you: How did your new life begin? Was it by working your heads off to please God? Or was it by responding to God's Message to you? Are you going to continue this craziness? For only crazy people would think they could complete by their own efforts what was begun by God. If you weren't smart enough or strong enough to begin it, how do you suppose you could perfect it?* (Galatians 3:1-3)

---

| *Uplifting* | *Discouraging* |
|---|---|
| ➢ | ➢ |
| ➢ | ➢ |
| ➢ | ➢ |

## *Our Work is Easy*

How does God perfect the new life he began in us? When the citizens of Colosse were struggling with this, Paul explained how:

*As you learn more and more how God works, you will learn how to do your work. We pray that you'll have the strength to stick it out over the long haul—not the grim strength of gritting your teeth but the glory-strength God gives. It is strength that endures the unendurable and spills over into joy, thanking the Father who makes us strong enough to take part in everything bright and beautiful that he has for us.* (Colossians 1:11-12)

These verses can be tricky to comprehend unless we learn how God designed our brain. Until we recognize that God designed the thinking side of our brain for his use, we are clueless how to do "our work." As these verses tell us, our work is not gritting our teeth. Gritting our teeth comes from doing our own thinking. God's job is thinking for us. Our job is to take part in everything bright and beautiful that he has for us. The way we take part in everything bright and beautiful is sensory focus on God. We give the attention of our five senses to God's bright and beautiful creation that surrounds us. We also give our sensory attention to God's Spirit in us. When we tune in through sensory focus to God's Spirit in us, we hear God's voice share his bright and beautiful thoughts.

| *Uplifting* | *Discouraging* |
|---|---|
| ➢ | ➢ |
| ➢ | ➢ |
| ➢ | ➢ |

These verses also highlight that "the joy of the Lord is my strength." We experience this joy even during seemingly unendurable circumstances. During these times, this joy is so strong that we can still see everything bright and beautiful that God has for us. God gives us such clear vision that we thank him for giving us strength. We don't credit ourselves. We follow what's written in the Proverbs 4:25-27:

*Keep your eyes straight ahead;*
 *ignore all sideshow distractions.*
*Watch your step,*
 *and the road will stretch out smooth before you.*
*Look neither right nor left;*
 *leave evil in the dust.*

Proverbs 4:20-22 also describes the upshot of leaving evil in the dust by keeping our eyes straight ahead:

*Dear friend, listen well to my words;*
 *tune your ears to my voice.*
*Keep my message in plain view at all times.*
 *Concentrate! Learn it by heart!*
*Those who discover these words live, really live;*
 *body and soul, they're bursting with health.*

These verses clearly indicate that a vital part of keeping our eyes straight ahead and ignoring all sideshow distractions is to have God's Word in plain view at all times. When you consider all these verses at the same time, sensory focus on

| *Uplifting* | *Discouraging* |
|---|---|
| ➢ | ➢ |
| ➢ | ➢ |
| ➢ | ➢ |

God stands out as the common theme. "Looking" straight ahead and "listening" to his words are the "work" God assigns to us. He gives us an assignment that everyone can do without any performance pressure to think for ourselves. I am thankful to be retired from my long career of thinking for myself.

| Uplifting | Discouraging |
|---|---|
| ➢ | ➢ |
| ➢ | ➢ |
| ➢ | ➢ |

| Uplifting | Discouraging |
| --- | --- |
| ➢ | ➢ |
| ➢ | ➢ |
| ➢ | ➢ |

## *Unconditional Love*

With such simple instructions like "Look and Listen" and "Focus and Follow", what is God's ultimate plan for those of us who accept his free offer to run our lives? His plan is to give us eternal life. That's how much God loves us:

> *This is how much God loved the world: He gave his Son, his one and only Son. And this is why: so that no one need be destroyed; by believing in him, anyone can have a whole and lasting life. God didn't go to all the trouble of sending his Son merely to point an accusing finger, telling the world how bad it was. He came to help, to put the world right again. Anyone who trusts in him is acquitted...* (John 3:16-18)

In today's world, our culture and church are notorious for pointing an accusing finger but not helping to rescue anyone. If there is anyone in a position to point a finger, it is God. God created the world. God also created Adam and Eve. He offered to run their lives and promised them happiness. Regrettably, because Adam and Eve could not resist the temptation to run their own lives, they disrupted God's plan. However, rather than destroy mankind, God showed mercy and offered a plan of redemption. God still offers to run our lives. All he requires is that we confess our inability to self-govern and he will give us a second chance to let him take over. Same promise and same guarantee for happiness. That is

| *Uplifting* | *Discouraging* |
|---|---|
| ➢ | ➢ |
| ➢ | ➢ |
| ➢ | ➢ |

the true meaning of unconditional love. Only God can love the world like that. God simply wants us—his followers—to encourage others to let God love them like he loves us. God wants his love in us to compel us to love others like God loves us:

> *If you've gotten anything at all out of following Christ, if his love has made any difference in your life, if being in a community of the Spirit means anything to you, if you have a heart, if you care— then do me a favor: Agree with each other, love each other, be deep-spirited friends. Don't push your way to the front; don't sweet-talk your way to the top. Put yourself aside, and help others get ahead. Don't be obsessed with getting your own advantage. Forget yourselves long enough to lend a helping hand.* (Philippians 2:1-4)

It is our own thoughts that are obsessed with getting our own way. Our own thoughts are incapable of forgetting ourselves. Our own thoughts will not allow us to lend a helping hand. Fortunately, God designed our brain so we could escape our own thinking. Only God's thoughts in us allow us to show others the love God has shown us.

| *Uplifting* | *Discouraging* |
|---|---|
| ➤ | ➤ |
| ➤ | ➤ |
| ➤ | ➤ |

## *Everyone Has a Plan*

To finally come to understand and accept that it is impossible for any good to come out of my defective thinking saved my life. This enlightenment came about for only one reason: I studied the Bible and learned how God made my brain. Both pieces were absolutely necessary for me to fully accept God's plan for my life. This plan is so simple and yet so miraculous. And it is the same plan for everyone. God invites everyone to be saved by his grace and to share their own salvation with everyone else. This has become my sole purpose in life. If God could take a man who was killing his followers (Saul) and transform him into a man who would stop at nothing to proclaim God's plan of salvation (Paul), God certainly can transform you and me. The transformed Paul writes this to the new Christians in Corinth:

> *Our firm decision is to work from this focused center: One man died for everyone. That puts everyone in the same boat. He included everyone in his death so that everyone could also be included in his life, a resurrection life, a far better life than people ever lived on their own.*
>
> *Because of this decision we don't evaluate people by what they have or how they look. We looked at the Messiah that way once and got it all wrong, as you know. We certainly don't look at him that way anymore. Now we look inside, and what we see is that anyone united*

| *Uplifting* | *Discouraging* |
|---|---|
| ➢ | ➢ |
| ➢ | ➢ |
| ➢ | ➢ |

*with the Messiah gets a fresh start, is created new. The old life is gone; a new life burgeons! Look at it! All this comes from the God who settled the relationship between us and him, and then called us to settle our relationships with each other. God put the world square with himself through the Messiah, giving the world a fresh start by offering forgiveness of sins. God has given us the task of telling everyone what he is doing. We're Christ's representatives. God uses us to persuade men and women to drop their differences and enter into God's work of making things right between them. We're speaking for Christ himself now: Become friends with God; he's already a friend with you.* (2 Cor. 5:14-20)

Paul uses the word "everyone" five times to emphasize that God wants everyone to join him in this new life. All of us have the same equal opportunity through our five senses ("work from this focused center" in verse 14) to be included in a "resurrection" life. God made all our brains in the same fashion so everyone has the same opportunity to let their own thinking die by way of a sensory "union" with God. It is not a cognitive union. It is our thoughts, not our senses, that are defective. God wants us to live in sensory harmony with him. This union empties our brain of our own thoughts. Only then does God have room to fill our brains with his thoughts. As more people enter into this FocusChoice life, we are not only united with God but with each other. We have "entered into God's work of making things right between

---

| *Uplifting* | *Discouraging* |
|---|---|
| ➢ | ➢ |
| ➢ | ➢ |
| ➢ | ➢ |

them." When others join us in sensory harmony with God, he brings us into cognitive harmony with each other, filling all of us with his thoughts. Our thoughts—divisive, argumentative, and filled with hate—are on the sidelines. With our thoughts out of commission, we are able to experience sensory love with God and each other.

| Uplifting | Discouraging |
|---|---|
| ➤ | ➤ |
| ➤ | ➤ |
| ➤ | ➤ |

|        Uplifting        |        Discouraging        |
| --- | --- |
| ➢ | ➢ |
| ➢ | ➢ |
| ➢ | ➢ |

## *God Doesn't Think Like Us*

I don't want my life to be about myself. I am not sure I ever did. It always made me nervous because of all the performance pressure. I just never knew how not to make life about myself. My best efforts always seemed to fail. From reading the Bible and learning how God made the brain, the "how" part has now become clear. When I am thinking for myself, my life is automatically about me. My cursed thoughts have no choice but to be selfish. Fortunately, God made my brain with the capacity to be filled with his thoughts rather than my own. This is why I want to be filled with God's thoughts:

> *Seek GOD while he's here to be found,*
>   *pray to him while he's close at hand.*
> *Let the wicked abandon their way of life*
>   *and the evil their way of thinking.*
> *Let them come back to GOD, who is merciful,*
>   *come back to our God, who is lavish with forgiveness.*
> *"I don't think the way you think.*
>   *The way you work isn't the way I work."*
>     *GOD's Decree.*
> *"For as the sky soars high above earth,*
>   *so the way I work surpasses the way you work,*
>   *and the way I think is beyond the way you think."*
>   (Isaiah 55:6-9)

---

*Uplifting*                    *Discouraging*

➤                              ➤


➤                              ➤


➤                              ➤

I learned the hard way throughout my life that thinking for myself does not work. I am relieved to learn the Bible says God's way of thinking and working is far superior to my own way. However, no one ever taught me how to access God's thinking. Even today, teaching within the church may oppose the truth that God wants to think for us, despite what God clearly teaches us in his Word.

Phillip Cary wrote the following words in his article entitled, "Is This God's Voice or Mine?"[7]:

> The practice of listening for God's voice in your heart is a very new development and it's deeply flawed. It has only recently displaced Scripture as the most important way, in the view of many Christians, that God reveals Himself to us, thanks in no small part to widespread promotion of the idea by otherwise evangelical churches and youth groups.

Although I keep my Bible right next to me all the time, I depend 100% on what God says to me each minute of every day. This is not new thinking and is certainly not flawed thinking. God gave these instructions long ago in the Bible to keep our focus on him nonstop so he can think for us nonstop. What is terribly flawed is no one has ever taught anyone how God designed our brain. Because courses on the brain have not been offered in theology schools, even well-trained theologians have no clue how God made the brain.

---

| *Uplifting* | *Discouraging* |
|---|---|
| ➢ | ➢ |
| ➢ | ➢ |
| ➢ | ➢ |

## *Whose Voice Do You Hear?*

What is the answer to the question in the title of Phillip Cary's article, "Is This God's Voice or Mine?"[7] We, the "experts" in our modern-day culture and church, think too much and do our very best to complicate God's Word. To be sure, distinguishing God's voice from our own is very easy—our voice is negative, God's voice is positive. Unlike secular therapies that promote replacing our own negative thoughts with our own (flawed) positive ones, FocusChoice Therapy recognizes that all uplifting thoughts are from God. Mankind is not capable of positive thinking on his or her own. How quickly we forget all human thoughts were cursed following the original sin of Adam and Eve eating from the tree of knowledge in the Garden of Eden, from Genesis 3:17-19:

> *Because you listened to your wife*
>    *and ate from the tree*
> *That I commanded you not to eat from,*
>    *'Don't eat from this tree,'*
> *The very ground is cursed because of you;*
>    *getting food from the ground*
> *Will be as painful as having babies is for your wife;*
>    *you'll be working in pain all your life long.*
> *The ground will sprout thorns and weeds,*
>    *you'll get your food the hard way,*
> *Planting and tilling and harvesting,*
>    *sweating in the fields from dawn to dusk,*

| *Uplifting* | *Discouraging* |
|---|---|
| ➤ | ➤ |
| ➤ | ➤ |
| ➤ | ➤ |

## The Bible and the Brain   111

*Until you return to that ground yourself, dead and buried;*

*you started out as dirt, you'll end up dirt.*

When I look at these verses through the lens of how God designed the brain, we are specifically being told that all descendants from Adam and Eve will be cursed in their thinking until the day they die. That means every one of us has screwed-up thoughts for as long as we live. Our only salvation is to give our sensory focus to God to be able to hear his thoughts while ours stay on the sidelines. When we hear our own evil thoughts, it should be a reminder to draw closer to God with our five senses.

That is why the Bible instructs us to always keep God's Word in plain view. Everything God tells us will line up with his Word. Since God never stops talking to us, we feel the need to have his Word close by to confirm what he is saying. Thank goodness for cell phones, tablets, and laptops! They allow us to google what the Bible says, in any translation.

Recently, a client wanted to argue with me that reading God's Word was a cognitive experience rather than a sensory one. The client contended it is a cognitive experience when we try to figure out what God is saying. However, God does not want us to think for ourselves or try to figure out what he is saying in his Word. God simply wants us to read with our eyes and receive what he says with our ears. Reading the Bible is no different than any other sensory experience with God. We simply focus with our senses and follow what he says.

---

| *Uplifting* | *Discouraging* |
|---|---|
| ➤ | ➤ |
| ➤ | ➤ |
| ➤ | ➤ |

## God's Voice is Not Anxious

Phillip Cary[7] expressed concern that people get anxious when they try to distinguish God's voice from their own. His point was we don't have to be anxious because God only speaks to us through his Word. Cary said God does not speak directly to our heart. It is true we don't have to be anxious. However, our own thoughts always produce anxiety. The solution is to keep our sensory attention on God at all times so our voice is silent. Then, we can hear God's direct voice reach our heart in countless ways. His voice is what removes our anxiety. God's voice drives me to the Bible, not as in "I should" read his Word but rather "I want to" read his Word. Listening to his thoughts in my brain is not a substitute for reading the Bible, and vice versa. When I live in the moment with my five senses on God, I get excited because I can count on his direct thoughts to me being confirmed in his Word. I feel very special that God wants to tell me what to think directly through his holy Spirit, and then, I find the same instructions in his Word. God wants every one of us to feel special in this way. Some theologians argue that "special" men of God heard his voice in the past but that kind of special treatment no longer exists. This self-thinking is contradictory to what has been revealed by God through his Word.

| *Uplifting* | *Discouraging* |
|---|---|
| ➢ | ➢ |
| ➢ | ➢ |
| ➢ | ➢ |

If God did not talk to us and think for us, the Bible would have never been written. Why would God no longer treat us in that same special way today? God designed our brains so he could think for us. God has not changed his design for our brain since his original creation. Even though Adam and Eve chose to think for themselves and cursed human thinking forever, God gives us an escape from our own thinking through sensory focus on him. God still offers us the sensory Garden of Eden, just like he did for Adam and Eve. But, just like Adam and Eve, God gives us a choice—rely on our own flawed thinking or rely on God's thoughts through sensory focus on him.

| *Uplifting* | *Discouraging* |
|---|---|
| ➢ | ➢ |
| ➢ | ➢ |
| ➢ | ➢ |

## *The Problem Solver*

When I use my God-given sensory freedom to focus the attention of my five senses on him, God has the freedom to fill my mind with his thoughts and the freedom to make me behave in a way that pleases him. We are a slave to whatever we place our sensory focus on. I am happy to be God's slave! I was miserable when I focused on my own thoughts, and I was a slave to them. I did not know how to break free from them. My own thoughts still make me feel miserable. But, now that I have learned how God made my brain, I can escape my thoughts by focusing my sensory attention to him. Learning how God made my brain has been life-changing for me in a big way. When I discovered that God can think for me while I center my five senses on him, my life was turned upside down in a wonderful way. Knowing God wants to think for me has fueled a fire in me to read the Bible every chance I get. Knowing he is thinking for me and working 24/7 on my behalf is a huge boost when I am in the middle of hard times and the world is crashing down all around me. At this point, I can't imagine dealing with difficult life situations on my own. Before I knew how God worked through my brain, I would cling to my own thoughts during hardships. I would worry and obsess nonstop, as if that would help me solve my problems. My worry was just an illusion that kept me focused on a problem that my own thinking could never begin to solve.

| *Uplifting* | *Discouraging* |
|---|---|
| ➤ | ➤ |
| ➤ | ➤ |
| ➤ | ➤ |

What a relief to learn how God solves all my problems:

> *I call to God;*
>   *God will help me.*
> *At dusk, dawn, and noon I sigh*
>   *deep sighs—he hears, he rescues.*
> *My life is well and whole, secure*
>   *in the middle of danger*
> *Even while thousands*
>   *are lined up against me.*
> *God hears it all, and from his judge's bench*
>   *puts them in their place.* (Psalm 55:16-18)

| *Uplifting* | *Discouraging* |
|---|---|
| ➢ | ➢ |
| ➢ | ➢ |
| ➢ | ➢ |

## *Easy Times*

After they let their old ways of thinking creep back in, Paul told the Galatians how simple and clear it is to grasp the radical difference between God's instructions on how to live and what happens when we follow our own thinking instead of God's:

> *It is obvious what kind of life develops out of trying to get your own way all the time: repetitive, loveless, cheap sex; a stinking accumulation of mental and emotional garbage; frenzied and joyless grabs for happiness; trinket gods; magic-show religion; paranoid loneliness; cutthroat competition; all-consuming-yet-never-satisfied wants; a brutal temper; an impotence to love or be loved; divided homes and divided lives; small-minded and lopsided pursuits; the vicious habit of depersonalizing everyone into a rival; uncontrolled and uncontrollable addictions; ugly parodies of community. I could go on.*
>
> *This isn't the first time I have warned you, you know. If you use your freedom this way, you will not inherit God's kingdom.*
>
> *But what happens when we live God's way? He brings gifts into our lives, much the same way that fruit appears in an orchard—things like affection for others, exuberance about life, serenity. We develop a*

| *Uplifting* | *Discouraging* |
|---|---|
| ➤ | ➤ |
| ➤ | ➤ |
| ➤ | ➤ |

*willingness to stick with things, a sense of compassion in the heart, and a conviction that a basic holiness permeates things and people. We find ourselves involved in loyal commitments, not needing to force our way in life, able to marshal and direct our energies wisely.* (Galatians 5:19-23)

The difference is huge when comparing the outcome of God thinking for us and following his Way with how we live when we think for ourselves. As awful as it sounds, the outcome of living my life based on my own thinking is identical to what is described in these verses. I could have checked every box on the terrible behavior list; and, as it said, "I could go on." I had been warned many times not to use my freedom this way, but I still felt like a slave to my own screw-ups. Thankfully, I finally learned how God designed the brain and discovered that the "freedom" these verses were describing was the opposite of what I had been taught for many years. I was taught that the freedom to which this passage refers meant I was free to either obey or disobey God. The actual meaning refers to my freedom of choice to either keep my sensory focus on God or keep my focus on my own thinking. I finally learned that when I choose to think for myself, terrible behaviors are guaranteed outcomes. Only keeping my sensory focus on God and listening to his thoughts produce the amazing behaviors that God gives us as gifts for letting him think for us. I am so grateful God made my brain so he could think for me while I keep my five senses fixed on

| *Uplifting* | *Discouraging* |
|---|---|
| ➢ | ➢ |
| ➢ | ➢ |
| ➢ | ➢ |

him. That is a choice I am capable of making. I cannot control my own behaviors when I think for myself, but God made my brain so I can control what my eyes look at, my ears listen to, my hands touch, my nose smells, and my mouth tastes.

| *Uplifting* | *Discouraging* |
|---|---|
| ➢ | ➢ |
| ➢ | ➢ |
| ➢ | ➢ |

|   Uplifting   | Discouraging |
|---|---|
| ➤ | ➤ |
| ➤ | ➤ |
| ➤ | ➤ |

## *A Divine Think Tank*

Many experts in our culture and church miss the secret of sensory focus on God. In fact, most experts still have no clue how God made the brain. They continue to place heavy emphasis on our own thinking. They instruct everyone to change their thinking. But the fact remains that our own thinking only changes for the worse as we pile up more and more negative thoughts. Any mental effort on our part to flip our thoughts to positive simply triggers additional thoughts of negativity. God did not design our brain to produce positive thoughts on its own. God made our brain to receive his thoughts when we dwell in sensory focus on him. Plain and simple, no short cuts or bypasses. Paul wrote to the Corinthians:

> *I want you to live as free of complications as possible. ...I'm trying to be helpful and make it as easy as possible for you, not make things harder. All I want is for you to be able to develop a way of life in which you can spend plenty of time together with the Master without a lot of distractions.* (1 Corinthians 7:32a, 35)

We continually make the conscious choice to maintain our sensory focus on God while he inputs his thoughts into our think tank. He does not mix his thoughts with ours in the think tank. Through sensory focus on God, our think tank is drained of our own thoughts. Any secular or Christian expert who

| *Uplifting* | *Discouraging* |
|---|---|
| ➢ | ➢ |
| ➢ | ➢ |
| ➢ | ➢ |

proposes that we have the capability to change our own cursed thoughts is not following what God tells in the Bible, and is clearly not yet aware of God's design for our brain.

It may seem like a technical distinction, but this distinction makes all the difference in the world. For the most part, secular and Christian experts agree that our thoughts are the problem. They lecture that our thoughts need to be different, that our negative thoughts can and need to be replaced by positive thoughts. However, both secular and Christian authors have missed the miracle of how our thoughts are transformed. We cannot change our thoughts on our own. We cannot make something good out of bad. That is voodoo. Some experts say that God helps us to change our thoughts from negative to positive. God does not help us do anything. He does it all on his own. God gets rid of our flawed thoughts and replaces them with his flawless thoughts. He takes our thoughts out of the starting lineup and relegates them to the bench. But God can do this only when we let him be our coach by devoting our sensory loyalty to him.

| *Uplifting* | *Discouraging* |
|---|---|
| ➤ | ➤ |
| ➤ | ➤ |
| ➤ | ➤ |

## *Turn Your Eyes Upon Jesus*

That God would think for me through the miracle of how he made my brain is totally counterintuitive. But, I am forever grateful that God thinks for me. I am relieved that he takes my thoughts out of the game and puts them on the sidelines. God's thoughts are brilliant and supernatural. He can accomplish things in and through me that are way out of my league. Things way beyond my wildest imaginations. God has brought me incredible joy. I cannot thank him enough! However, once in a while, sometimes on a daily basis, my thoughts jump off the bench and run back in the game. God runs my life so smoothly that sometimes, when there is clear sailing, my own thoughts trick me into believing I deserve the credit for being happy. How quickly my own thoughts interfere with my happiness! If I take my eyes (and other four senses) off the coach for a split second, my thoughts run back onto the court. I used to beat myself up for rebounding back to my own thoughts. Now, as soon as I do something stupid on the court, I look over to my coach. With such compassion in his eyes, he immediately offers to rescue me from further embarrassment. And, he doesn't embarrass me as my thoughts slink their way back to the bench. He simply loves on me and tells me:

> I understand. You've been playing your own game for 60 years. It takes time and practice to totally embrace the idea of me thinking for you and running your life.

| *Uplifting* | *Discouraging* |
|---|---|
| ➤ | ➤ |
| ➤ | ➤ |
| ➤ | ➤ |

You have very little experience following me. I am not asking for perfection. I am only asking that you make the simple choice to put you sensory attention on me. That requires no mental effort, no thinking at all on your part. Otherwise, that would make my design for the brain useless. My design for the brain was to allow me to think for you. I do not want you to think. Period!

Sensory focus does not require human thinking at all. God made the sensory brain so we can turn our eyes, move our body, smell a different scent, listen to a different voice, and taste a different flavor without any human effort whatsoever. Just a simple continuous, conscious choice to turn our eyes upon Jesus. The hymn "Turn Your Eyes Upon Jesus" (based on Hebrews 12:2, "Keep your eyes on Jesus, who both began and finished this race we're in"), written in 1922 by Helen H. Lemmel—who was blind at the time—says it best:

> O soul, are you weary and troubled?
> No light in the darkness you see?
> There's light for a look at the Savior,
> And life more abundant and free!
>
> Turn your eyes upon Jesus,
> Look full in His wonderful face,
> And the things of earth will grow strangely dim,
> In the light of His glory and grace.

---

| Uplifting | Discouraging |
|---|---|
| ➤ | ➤ |
| ➤ | ➤ |
| ➤ | ➤ |

Through death into life everlasting
He passed, and we follow Him there;
O'er us sin no more hath dominion—
For more than conqu'rors we are!

His Word shall not fail you—He promised;
Believe Him, and all will be well:
Then go to a world that is dying,
His perfect salvation to tell!

| Uplifting | Discouraging |
|---|---|
| ➢ | ➢ |
| ➢ | ➢ |
| ➢ | ➢ |

|  *Uplifting* | *Discouraging* |
|---|---|
| ➢ | ➢ |
| ➢ | ➢ |
| ➢ | ➢ |

## *Our Addiction of Choice*

The hymn "Turn Your Eyes Upon the Lord" portrays a wonderful life of believing in God through sensory focus on him. God promises that all will be well as he leads us to share a life of salvation with the world. Why does it take so long for many of us to follow this simple yet radical path? I believe we do follow a sensory path in our lives, but a sensory path to earthly addictions rather than a heavenly addiction. The sensory path to earthly addictions is quite simple but can also be uncompromising and life-threatening. It is an escape route from our own anxious and angry thoughts. I call this condition the Triple A Club: **A**ddictions are the guaranteed outcome of **A**nxious and **A**ngry thoughts. Our own thinking is guaranteed to take us down the path to disaster and depression. We have no choice but to turn to either earthly addictions or heavenly addiction. Even though we know earthly addictions will lead us farther down the path to more disaster and deeper depression, we simply have no mental strength through our own cursed thoughts to resist earthly addictions.

Earthly addictions are infinite in number. I learn about new ones every day. My most recent example is a client who hugs his cat so tightly until he squeezes all her air out and she makes that last breath sound. Then, he lets go before she suffocates. How could this behavior possibly qualify as an addiction? The chemical rush from such high-stakes risk-

| *Uplifting* | *Discouraging* |
|---|---|
| ➤ | ➤ |
| ➤ | ➤ |
| ➤ | ➤ |

taking is intoxicating. It outweighs any thoughts of harming a helpless animal. When we rely on our own thinking day in and day out, we are guaranteed frequent bouts of anxiety and anger. It is the natural outcome of thinking for ourselves. If no one has taught us that we can escape to God's thoughts, we have no choice but to succumb to myriad "pleasurable" earthly addictions. We desperately seek sensory relief from the barrage of our anxious and angry thoughts. This relief may be in the form of alcohol, drugs, medication, food, gambling, sex, porn, adultery, shopping, gaming, or a hefty menu of any number of worldly pleasures. They all have one thing in common: the release of pleasure chemicals that make us feel good. The pleasure is most certainly intense, but miserably short-lived. God is the inventor of such an amazing brain that can signal the human body to release chemicals that make us feel so good, for a long, long time. His plan is for us to escape to him so that this release of chemical pleasure will be used for his purposes.

| *Uplifting* | *Discouraging* |
|---|---|
| ➢ | ➢ |
| ➢ | ➢ |
| ➢ | ➢ |

## *Thought Addiction*

How is God's design to spread his love and happiness around the world connected to his framework for our brain's disposition toward heavenly addiction? As much as our brain can feel good and be devoted to earthly addictions, these addictions pale in comparison to the happiness we experience through a heavenly addiction to God. Earthly addictions make us feel good in the moment, but do not offer us the life of happiness that heavenly addiction delivers. Regrettably, the long-term consequence of earthly addictions is doom and gloom. For example, when we devote our five senses to food addiction or drug addiction, our thought life becomes consumed and obsessed with finding our next fix. Our mind is filled up with our food god or our drug god. We become a slave to those gods that command our sensory focus. While in this captivity, our mind is filled with thoughts about our god of choice. Our main obsession is our own thoughts. We are consumed by them. We are driven by them. And we can be destroyed by them, just like any other addiction. Our obsessive thoughts become our god.

We have only one avenue of escape. It is not having an empty mind. It is replacing our own cluttered, chaotic thoughts with God's thoughts. God wants our mind to be filled with his thoughts instead and being empty of our own thoughts. He offers one simple but guaranteed escape route. God gives all

| *Uplifting* | *Discouraging* |
|---|---|
| ➢ | ➢ |
| ➢ | ➢ |
| ➢ | ➢ |

of us the same brain capacity to turn our sensory focus to him, the one true God. Our sensory devotion to him leaves all our other false gods (including our own thought life) stranded by the side of the road. These false gods will dry up and blow away simply by continuously living in sensory time with God:

*We're all sin-infected, sin-contaminated.*
  *Our best efforts are grease-stained rags.*
*We dry up like autumn leaves—*
  *sin-dried, we're blown off by the wind.* (Isaiah 64:6)

Clearly, this description of our own thoughts tells us we all need an escape from our own minds. Our thinking is infected and contaminated by sin, cursed since the moment Adam and Eve ate the fruit of the tree of knowledge. I no longer want to have other gods before me. Me and my own thoughts are first in line to be cast aside through inviting God's thoughts into my life through my sensory obsession with him.

| *Uplifting* | *Discouraging* |
|---|---|
| ➢ | ➢ |
| ➢ | ➢ |
| ➢ | ➢ |

## *A Thought Transfusion*

How do we become obsessed with God and his thoughts? From a brain perspective, the process of becoming an addict to God's thoughts is no different than being an addict to our own thinking. Because of the sin of Adam and Eve, we are all born with the curse of being addicted to our own thinking. We need a total makeover. This makeover is not possible without making the choice to let God replace our thoughts with his thoughts. A holy makeover! How does the transfusion take place? In his book *Think Differently, Live Differently*[8], Bob Hamp gives a poetic description of this replacement process and how God wants to relate to us:

> God is with us. God is among His people. He wants to have a cup of coffee with you. He wants to drive to work with you, even when you don't want to drive to work. He wants to comfort you when you lose your favorite person, or any person for that matter. He doesn't just want to be involved in your circumstances, He wants to be engaged with your heart. The Father is with you at all times, no matter where you are or what you are doing, and He wants you to notice that He is there. More than just notice. He wants you to purposefully tune into His presence in these moments. (page 149)

| *Uplifting* | *Discouraging* |
|---|---|
| ➢ | ➢ |
| ➢ | ➢ |
| ➢ | ➢ |

In fact, God designed our brain so we can be in sensory presence with him every moment. How do we go from loyalty to our own thoughts to utter devotion to having his divine thoughts in us? What is the actual process of how God does this transformation? There is no room in the thinking cavity of our brain for both our thoughts and God's thoughts to be in operation at the same time. Our thoughts are rivals with God's thoughts. They oppose his thoughts. They are always louder than his thoughts:

> *Then he was told, "Go, stand on the mountain at attention before GOD. GOD will pass by."*
>
> *A hurricane wind ripped through the mountains and shattered the rocks before GOD, but GOD wasn't to be found in the wind; after the wind an earthquake, but GOD wasn't in the earthquake; and after the earthquake fire, but GOD wasn't in the fire; and after the fire a gentle and quiet whisper.* (1 Kings 19:11-12)

God's Holy divine thoughts cannot co-exist with our cursed thoughts. Our own thoughts drown out what God desires to share with us. Bob Hamp writes, "God wants to be engaged with our hearts." As I have said many times, God surrounds us with his presence and lives in us through his Holy Spirit. God desires that we embrace his presence on a continual basis. How do we purposefully tune into his presence so God can be engaged with our hearts? Using brain terminology, we tune into his presence in the same technical manner that we tune into our own thoughts or our own addictions or our own gods: sensory focus on God.

| *Uplifting* | *Discouraging* |
|---|---|
| ➢ | ➢ |
| ➢ | ➢ |
| ➢ | ➢ |

## God's Computer in Us

What actually happens when we tune into God's ongoing presence in our lives by giving him the attention of all five of our senses? We can embrace the truth that our brain is actually God's instrument in our lives to think for us, talk to us, talk for us to others, and take action in our lives. And we are inspired to purposefully give God the full, undivided attention of our five senses. After all, our senses are the entry point for input into God's computer in us—our brain. When we focus our five senses on God, it allows God to operate his computer that he tailor made specifically for us. How quickly many of us forget that we are each a masterpiece, individually and uniquely designed by God:

> *"Before I shaped you in the womb,*
> *I knew all about you.*
> *Before you saw the light of day,*
> *I had holy plans for you:*
> *A prophet to the nations—*
> *that's what I had in mind for you."*
> *But I said, "Hold it, Master GOD! Look at me.*
> *I don't know anything. I'm only a boy!"*
> *GOD told me, "Don't say, 'I'm only a boy.'*
> *I'll tell you where to go and you'll go there.*
> *I'll tell you what to say and you'll say it.*
> *Don't be afraid of a soul.*
> *I'll be right there, looking after you."*
> *GOD'S Decree. (Jeremiah 1:5-8)*

| *Uplifting* | *Discouraging* |
|---|---|
| ➢ | ➢ |
| ➢ | ➢ |
| ➢ | ➢ |

The Apple engineers who created Siri are brilliant, but not nearly as brilliant as God. Siri allows us to communicate with our iPhones ("Hey Siri…"). Since the beginning of time, God put a computer with his voice in the brain of every one of us. This is how we communicate with God ("Dear God…").

What does purposefully giving God the attention of our five senses look like in real time? Consider how our senses are brought to their peak when we ride a motorcycle. We experience the wind and the roar of the engine, we feel our hands gripping the handle bars, and we smell the aromas of the outdoors. However, when driving a quiet car, our senses can be lulled to sleep (except for closing our eyes, of course!). While driving a car, some of us, myself included, have spent almost a lifetime over-thinking to the extreme such that we miss turns and head in the wrong direction. Anytime we think for ourselves, not just in our car, we head in the direction of disaster. Once we accept that God crafted us into being and installed his brain in us to be used for his glory, we hunger for God to be our new voice. We want him to show us new ways, every day, to live at full sensory capacity.

---

| *Uplifting* | *Discouraging* |
|---|---|
| ➢ | ➢ |
| ➢ | ➢ |
| ➢ | ➢ |

## *Even Me*

God's loving and caring voice is the most incredible aspect of his presence in me. It is beyond my human comprehension that God is alive in me. Why would God love and care for me after I rejected his intended design for my life for so many years? And not just me; he wants to love and care for others through me. God wants even me as a carrier of his love. Again, that exceeds my humanly grasp. Although it took until I was 60 years old to learn how to embrace God's love through sensory focus, he was planting his voice in me when I was a child. Among the hymns we sang in Sunday School, I remember learning the words to "Jesus Loves Even Me," written by Philip P. Bliss in 1870:

> I am so glad that our Father in heaven,
> tells of His love in the Book He has written;
> Wonderful words in the Bible I see,
> this is the story that Jesus loves me.
>
>> I am so glad that Jesus loves me,
>> Jesus loves me, Jesus loves me.
>> I am so glad that Jesus loves me,
>> Jesus loves even me.
>
> Though I forget Him and wonder away,
> Still He doth love me wherever I stray;
> Back to His dear loving arms do I flee,
> When I remember that Jesus loves me.

| *Uplifting* | *Discouraging* |
|---|---|
| ➤ | ➤ |
| ➤ | ➤ |
| ➤ | ➤ |

Oh, if there's only one song I can sing,
When in His beauty I see the great King,
This shall my song through eternity be,
Oh, what a wonder that Jesus loves me!

What blows my mind is that God uses even me. God uses his love in me to introduce others to his magnificent love. Even when I find it impossible for me to love myself or others, God loves me and others through me:

> *So, chosen by God for this new life of love, dress in the wardrobe God picked out for you: compassion, kindness, humility, quiet strength, discipline. Be even-tempered, content with second place, quick to forgive an offense. Forgive as quickly and completely as the Master forgave you. And regardless of what else you put on, wear love. It's your basic, all-purpose garment. Never be without it.* (Colossians 3:12-14)

| *Uplifting* | *Discouraging* |
|---|---|
| ➤ | ➤ |
| ➤ | ➤ |
| ➤ | ➤ |

## *Wear Love*

When I read verses about love, like Colossians 3:12-14, my natural tendency is to feel a pressure to be loving. I was expected by my parents and the church to be loving since the time I was a little boy. In fact, I always felt defective with respect to love because I was told as a little boy I was difficult to love. I interpreted that to mean I was unlovable. I carried this self-fulfilling perception throughout my life. I know now, from learning how God made our brain, that our own thinking will always lead to self-hatred. This condition is a guaranteed outcome of our inherited cursed thoughts.

I have been so relieved to learn, after all these years, that God does not expect us to love ourselves or others through our own will power. If we could, we would not need God's love. God did not design our brain to yield love through its own thought engine. God is the engineer of love in our lives, both giving and receiving. When we choose to be attentive to God with our five senses, he produces the feeling of us being loved by him. How? The thoughts he generates in our brain yield the feeling of love in our hearts. That is why the verses in Colossians tell us God designs for us a wardrobe of love for us to wear. We attire ourselves in these magnificent garments of compassion, kindness, humility, quiet strength, and discipline by keeping our gaze on God with all our senses. We put on love that God produces in us. We cannot generate love on our own. The same beautiful wardrobe he chooses for us is the

| *Uplifting* | *Discouraging* |
|---|---|
| ➤ | ➤ |
| ➤ | ➤ |
| ➤ | ➤ |

same wardrobe that reveals to others his love in us. No self-thought is required on our part. In fact, mental effort on our part prevents us from feeling love. God only requires that we make the continuous, conscious choice of sensory focus on him:

> ...*[L]ove the Lord your God with all your passion and prayer and muscle and intelligence...* (Luke 10:27)

Any thoughts on our part interrupt our sensory concentration on God, thereby disrupting any feeling of love God wants to give us. We simply cannot put on God's wardrobe of love if we are locked into our own thinking.

| *Uplifting* | *Discouraging* |
|---|---|
| ➤ | ➤ |
| ➤ | ➤ |
| ➤ | ➤ |

## *Living in the Freedom of God*

We cannot give and receive love on our own. With that pressure shed from our lives, God comes through with an ongoing supply of new love for us every day. His love is both unexpected and irresistible to us and others in our lives. It is God's most amazing way of caring for the world he created and loves dearly. Without his love, God's followers around the world could never endure the terrible hate they suffer. Hatred fabricated by mankind's insistence on thinking for itself. You would think that these devastating results would drive everyone to God. Sadly, most people are clueless how God made our brain as his instrument to save the world through his love. Hopefully, this book will reach some of these people. My hope is this book will show people how God made the brain and show how he wants us to help carry out his plan for love to save the world:

Could it be any clearer? Our old way of life was nailed to the cross with Christ, a decisive end to that sin-miserable life—no longer at sin's every beck and call! What we believe is this: If we get included in Christ's sin-conquering death, we also get included in his life-saving resurrection. We know that when Jesus was raised from the dead it was a signal of the end of death-as-the-end. Never again will death have the last word. When Jesus died, he took sin down with him, but alive he brings God down to us. From now on, think of it this way: Sin speaks a dead language that means nothing to you; God speaks

| *Uplifting* | *Discouraging* |
|---|---|
| ➢ | ➢ |
| ➢ | ➢ |
| ➢ | ➢ |

your mother tongue, and you hang on every word. You are dead to sin and alive to God. That's what Jesus did.

> *That means you must not give sin a vote in the way you conduct your lives. Don't give it the time of day. Don't even run little errands that are connected with that old way of life. Throw yourselves wholeheartedly and full-time—remember, you've been raised from the dead!—into God's way of doing things. Sin can't tell you how to live. After all, you're not living under that old tyranny any longer. You're living in the freedom of God.*
> (Romans 6:6-14)

| *Uplifting* | *Discouraging* |
|---|---|
| ➢ | ➢ |
| ➢ | ➢ |
| ➢ | ➢ |

## *Pass along the Gift of God's Love*

Speaking of God sending new feelings of love every day, those verses from Romans 6 feel new to me. I probably glanced over them in the past. This morning, as I write, the verses take on a fireworks-type new meaning. When I read them through the lens of how God uses our brain as his instrument in us, God shared these thoughts with me to write down:

I used to live my life under the tyranny of my own cursed thoughts I inherited from Adam and Eve. Living under that tyranny, I was dead to God's voice and his love. I could not hear his voice no matter how I tried. Through God's plan of salvation, I received Christ into my life and I follow him through sensory focus without trying at all. I have been raised from the dead into God's way of doing things. My thoughts have been nailed to the cross with Christ. His death put an end to living under the tyranny of my own thinking. When Jesus died, he took the curse of my sinful thoughts down with him. But, Christ arose from the dead. He is alive again and he brings God down to me. My sinful thoughts are a dead language that mean nothing to me. Now, God speaks my mother tongue. He is my new voice. He speaks to me in English. I hang onto his every word. God taking over and thinking for me means I am no longer at the beck and call of my own sinful thoughts. I am now living in the freedom of God thinking for me.

| *Uplifting* | *Discouraging* |
|---|---|
| ➢ | ➢ |
| ➢ | ➢ |
| ➢ | ➢ |

I stay busy keeping my five senses on God all the time. I know this sensory focus keeps me living in the freedom of God thinking for me. Whenever I have nothing to do in the moment, my favorite way to keep my sensory connection with God is through reading his Word and sharing the thoughts God gives me through writing books. I feel so special and experience God's love in a deep way I never thought possible. I love to receive his love in this way. My favorite gift of love from God is how his voice shares new words with me on a continual basis. My desire is to pass on this gift of God's love to you. I trust you will feel God's love like I have. I trust his words will be new and fresh to you every day.

| *Uplifting* | *Discouraging* |
|---|---|
| ➤ | ➤ |
| ➤ | ➤ |
| ➤ | ➤ |

## *Don't Give Your Thoughts a Vote*

God's love feels fresh and new every day. Despite this wonderful gift, I have found one thing that can interrupt or interfere with a loving sensory relationship with God—high stress. Many of my FocusChoice clients and I tend to accuse ourselves of failure during high-stress moments, which may last days or even weeks. The fact remains that God says in his Word these tough times will not disappear as we experience a close, loving relationship with him through sensory focus. If anything, we may experience even more trouble the closer we walk with God. Why? Certainly not because God desires that we struggle. God's divine wisdom knows his sensory followers do not fit well within a fallen world. Most people continue to operate as if they are better than God at running their own lives. As long as we continue to think for themselves, we will continue to be surrounded by hatred, the guaranteed outcome of living based in our own cursed thoughts. In the first his two letters, Peter, the rock of the Christ's church, tells us what to do when—not if—life gets stressful:

> *Friends, when life gets really difficult, don't jump to the conclusion that God isn't on the job. Instead, be glad that you are in the very thick of what Christ experienced. This is a spiritual refining process, with glory just around the corner.*

| *Uplifting* | *Discouraging* |
|---|---|
| ➤ | ➤ |
| ➤ | ➤ |
| ➤ | ➤ |

*If you're abused because of Christ, count yourself fortunate. It's the Spirit of God and his glory in you that brought you to the notice of others. If they're on you because you broke the law or disturbed the peace, that's a different matter. But if it's because you're a Christian, don't give it a second thought. Be proud of the distinguished status reflected in that name!* (1 Peter 4:12-16)

Peter makes it clear—all of us who keep our full sensory attention on Christ will encounter difficult times. These difficult times are a reminder that our loyalty to Christ will put us in the thick of the same suffering that Christ himself experienced. This suffering causes a lot of sinful noise to swirl in our minds. This noise can quickly intensify and interfere with our senses abilities to tune into God's voice. Yet, God's voice is the only answer to feeling peace in the midst of trouble. In fact, Paul told the Romans to not give our voice a single vote; not give our voice the time of day; not even run little errands for our own voice. These little errands would just re-connect us to our old sinful voice.

How do we closely tune into God's voice and block out all the noise of sin that surrounds us? How do we not tune back into our own sinful voice upon which we relied for all those years? We increase our sensory concentration. As Paul said, we hang on God's every word. We throw ourselves wholeheartedly and full-time into God's voice. In brain language, how does that work? I remember constantly being

| *Uplifting* | *Discouraging* |
|---|---|
| ➢ | ➢ |
| ➢ | ➢ |
| ➢ | ➢ |

surrounded by deafening noise. To block the noise, I carried 3x5 cards of uplifting verses in my pocket to look at every moment my mind was free. When I didn't do this, my mind would automatically return to worry. Sometimes, on my way home from work, the music I'm playing steps out of the background; I tune in more closely to the drum beat and sing the words with passion!

| *Uplifting* | *Discouraging* |
|---|---|
| ➤ | ➤ |
| ➤ | ➤ |
| ➤ | ➤ |

|  Uplifting  |  Discouraging  |
| --- | --- |
| ➤ | ➤ |
| ➤ | ➤ |
| ➤ | ➤ |

## *God's Strong, Gentle Voice*

God's voice is our only hope to drown out our own voice and all the voices of the world. God gives us countless ways to turn up the sensory volume to intensify our focus on him. However, and perhaps most importantly, sensory volume and hearing God's voice are not about loudness. The world's voice is loud and hateful. God's voice is gentle and can be heard through countless sensory avenues. Before my clients even learn that it is God's voice they are hearing, they share with me how God is trying to reach them. One client listens to Christmas music in July because it makes her feel warm inside. That is God making her feel warm. Another client loves to walk her dog in the autumn air when the leaves have fallen to the ground. The rustling leaves relax her on weekends when she wants a breather away from her high-stress job during the week. God's voice is heard in the sound of the rustling leaves. I learned this about God's voice by reading the Psalms:

> GOD, *brilliant Lord,*
>    *yours is a household name.*
> *Nursing infants gurgle choruses about you;*
>    *toddlers shout the songs*
> *That drown out enemy talk,*
>    *and silence atheist babble.*
> *I look up at your macro-skies, dark and enormous,*
>    *your handmade sky-jewelry,*
> *Moon and stars mounted in their settings.*

| *Uplifting* | *Discouraging* |
|---|---|
| ➢ | ➢ |
| ➢ | ➢ |
| ➢ | ➢ |

*GOD, brilliant Lord,*
   *your name echoes around the world.* (Psalm 8:1-3,9)

God is so brilliant that he showcases his voice in a million ways. I never knew the countless expressions of his voice until I began to read the Bible closely and study how God made the brain. I am so thankful that God equipped my human brain as his instrument to share his voice. These verses describe my own voice and the voices of the world as being enemy, atheist babble. What a blessing that God made the human brain so there is a way to escape our own thoughts and the thoughts of the world. Like many of my clients and readers, I reached the end of the rope by constantly listening to my own angry, anxious, and addictive thoughts. They completely wore me out! God showed me how to let him rescue me. Like David wrote in the Psalms, my sensory focus began as crying:

*I'm tired of all this—so tired. My bed*
   *has been floating forty days and nights*
*On the flood of my tears.*
   *My mattress is soaked, soggy with tears.*
*The sockets of my eyes are black holes;*
   *nearly blind, I squint and grope.*
*Get out of here, you Devil's crew:*
   *at last GOD has heard my sobs.*
*My requests have all been granted,*
   *my prayers are answered.*
*Cowards, my enemies disappear.*
*Disgraced, they turn tail and run.* (Psalm 6:6-10)

---

| *Uplifting* | *Discouraging* |
|---|---|
| ➢ | ➢ |
| ➢ | ➢ |
| ➢ | ➢ |

Thank God that he made my brain with an escape route from my cowardly and disgraced thoughts so he could fill the vacated space with his thoughts. My thoughts are my enemy. My only choice is for God to think for me. God continually thinks for all of us, but we won't hear his thoughts until we run to him for refuge. God does not enjoy one minute of our suffering. Everyone seems to think God waits until the last minute to rescue us. Quite the opposite! It is we who wait until the last minute to run to God with our sensory focus.

| *Uplifting* | *Discouraging* |
|---|---|
| ➤ | ➤ |
| ➤ | ➤ |
| ➤ | ➤ |

|       Uplifting       |      Discouraging      |
| --------------------- | ---------------------- |
| ➢                     | ➢                      |
| ➢                     | ➢                      |
| ➢                     | ➢                      |

## *God's Safe-House*

I have many examples of how we wait until the last minute to run to God with our sensory focus. We often allow our own defective thoughts to drive us to an emotional state of complete panic. One client shared with me that her heart raced, her hands trembled, she felt like she was going to throw up, she had dry-heaves, she could not sleep, and her whole body felt frozen. She was terrified by her symptoms and petrified by how she felt. To use her words, she was "freaking out." Because of how she felt, she could see why some people cut themselves to relocate their pain. She also feared she might get to the point of feeling suicidal if her pain got any worse. Many people do cut themselves and many people do feel suicidal. Some even attempt suicide. Some succeed. Our own cursed thoughts certainly do have the potential to kill us.

David would frequently get to the point of total despair in how he felt:

*God, listen to me shout,*
    *bend an ear to my prayer.*
*When I'm far from anywhere,*
    *down to my last gasp,*
*I call out, "Guide me*
    *up High Rock Mountain!"* (Psalm 61:1-2)

---

| *Uplifting* | *Discouraging* |
|---|---|
| ➤ | ➤ |
| ➤ | ➤ |
| ➤ | ➤ |

This is a perfect description of how our brain works. Our own thoughts take us far from anywhere and down to our last gasp. Unfortunately, many of us do not call out to God before we reach this point of desperation. In the same chapter of Psalms, David tells us the good that happens when we cry out to God:

*You've always given me breathing room,*
  *a place to get away from it all,*
*A lifetime pass to your safe-house,*
  *an open invitation as your guest.*
*You've always taken me seriously, God,*
  *made me welcome among those who know and love you.*
(Psalm 61:3-5)

We have assurance from God that he will always give us the freedom to breathe. He gives us an open, continual invitation to his safe-house. From the perspective of our brain, God's safe-house is where we go when we give him the total attention of our five senses. We rely entirely on God's voice instead of our own. The Psalms tell us God wants us to rely on him for a lifetime.

| *Uplifting* | *Discouraging* |
|---|---|
| ➢ | ➢ |
| ➢ | ➢ |
| ➢ | ➢ |

## *A Basket of Stress*

Despite God's lifetime guarantee, why did I wait until I was 60 years old to choose to continually rely on God rather than sporadically and only when I was down to my last gasp? This is the million-dollar question to which we all want the answer. I cannot answer for anyone else. Speaking for myself, I never understood how God could actually speaks for us. Without making any excuses, I never gave the Bible my full sensory attention. In fact, I didn't understand what sensory focus was until I studied how God made the brain. God gave me full understanding when I simply devoted my sensory attention to him through ongoing study of the Bible and the brain. God's voice gives me new insight every time I study. I practice this study every time my mind is tempted to worry. For me, every time is all the time. My mind was pre-programmed to worry about everything. God has re-programmed my mind to re-set my focus on him and listen to his voice rather than my own anxious voice. One client described her life as a "basket of stress." At age 26, she even questioned whether God had a plan for her life. That description applies to all of us regardless of our age. We are all doomed to a lifetime of stress if we rely on our own thinking and our own voice.

David felt his life was a basket of stress. He always seemed to be surrounded by enemies:

| *Uplifting* | *Discouraging* |
|---|---|
| ➢ | ➢ |
| ➢ | ➢ |
| ➢ | ➢ |

*And me? I pray.*
*God, it's time for a break!*

*God, answer in love!*
*Answer with your sure salvation!*

*Rescue me from the swamp,*
*Don't let me go under for good,*

*Pull me out of the clutch of the enemy;*
*This whirlpool is sucking me down.*

*Don't let the swamp be my grave, the Black Hole*
*Swallow me, its jaws clenched around me.*

*Now answer me, God, because you love me;*
*Let me see your great mercy full-face.*

*Don't look the other way; your servant can't take it.*
*I'm in trouble. Answer right now!*

*Come close, God; get me out of here.*
*Rescue me from this deathtrap.* (Psalm 69:13-18)

David's feelings are an accurate description of how we all feel when we rely on our own thinking. Like David, God wants us to share our stinkin' thinkin' with him. It marks the beginning of turning to God and giving him our sensory focus so he can replace our negative thoughts with his uplifting thoughts. David's thoughts in these verses were loaded with negativity. The whirlpool of his thoughts was sucking him

---

| *Uplifting* | *Discouraging* |
|---|---|
| ➢ | ➢ |
| ➢ | ➢ |
| ➢ | ➢ |

down into a swamp, a grave, a black hole. We can often feel like David, where our thoughts put us in a black hole that has us in the clench of its jaws and wants to swallow us up. We get so negative that we feel God might let us go under for good. We become afraid that God does not love us and will not rescue us from our thoughts, which are our enemy. We cry out to God because we can't bear the mental pain of our own thoughts any longer.

| *Uplifting* | *Discouraging* |
|---|---|
| ➢ | ➢ |
| ➢ | ➢ |
| ➢ | ➢ |

|   Uplifting   |   Discouraging   |
| --- | --- |
| ➤ | ➤ |
| ➤ | ➤ |
| ➤ | ➤ |

## *God, You've Done It All!*

David cries out to God in Psalm 69:29:

*I'm hurt and in pain;*
*Give me space for healing, and mountain air.*

Immediately, God speaks to David. God's voice tells David, and all of us, how to give him our sensory attention:

*Let me shout God's name with a praising song,*
*Let me tell his greatness in a prayer of thanks.*

*For GOD, this is better than oxen on the altar,*
*Far better than blue-ribbon bulls.*

*The poor in spirit see and are glad—*
*Oh, you God-seekers, take heart!*

*For GOD listens to the poor,*
*He doesn't walk out on the wretched.*

*You heavens, praise him; praise him, earth;*
*Also ocean and all things that swim in it.*

*For God is out to help Zion,*
*Rebuilding the wrecked towns of Judah.*

*Guess who will live there—*
*The proud owners of the land?*

*No, the children of his servants will get it,*
*The lovers of his name will live in it.* (Psalm 69:30-36)

| *Uplifting* | *Discouraging* |
|---|---|
| ➢ | ➢ |
| ➢ | ➢ |
| ➢ | ➢ |

When we cry out to God with our five senses, he talks to us. He gives us songs to praise him and prayers to lift up to him. God gives us a thankful heart because he always listens to our pain and never walks out on us. Instead, God points our five senses to the heavens that praise him, and to the earth and the oceans that praise him, too. We feel God's presence. He tells us he will help us and rebuild our lives. God assures us that those who love him will live in his presence.

Once we choose to live continually in the moment with God through maintaining our sensory focus on him, God uses us to share with others what he has taught us:

*You got me when I was an unformed youth,*
*God, and taught me everything I know.*

*Now I'm telling the world your wonders;*
*I'll keep at it until I'm old and gray.*

*God, don't walk off and leave me*
*until I get out the news*

*Of your strong right arm to this world,*
*news of your power to the world yet to come,*

*Your famous and righteous*
*ways, O God.*

*God, you've done it all!* (Psalm 71:17-20)

---

*Uplifting*          *Discouraging*

➤          ➤

➤          ➤

➤          ➤

## *Living in Bondage*

Once I learned how God wants to use my brain as his instrument to speak to me and to run my life, sharing this incredible news with everyone became my passion. I want others to know that God has done it all in my life. Sharing this news keeps my sensory focus on God, which means he will do even more in and through me. I delight in being God's slave. I hated being my own slave because my results were disastrous. I was so miserable and felt dead inside. And the pressure I felt to perform paralyzed me from accomplishing anything. Now, I feel so loved that God desires to do a great work in and through me. There is nothing else that I would rather be doing at this point in my life. God makes me feel so important. Yet, I feel absolutely no pressure to accomplish anything at a personal level. I do not desire any credit. I love to give God all the credit because I know that only God has earned the credit. I know I cannot handle personal success. God did not design my brain to be successful on its own. No wonder I have been a mess all these years. I never knew any better. I thought it was my responsibility to become a success in life. That was never God's plan from the time of creation. He knew no man or woman could handle success on their own. That is why he designed every brain to only experience success with God as the operator.

| *Uplifting* | *Discouraging* |
|---|---|
| ➢ | ➢ |
| ➢ | ➢ |
| ➢ | ➢ |

I am well aware that being God's slave is not a popular teaching in today's world, even among Christians. We pride ourselves in being independent operators of our own lives. The crux of church teaching is to be the best that we can be in our efforts to be a good Christian. The so-called "good" Christian carries more pressure to perform than anyone else. Because God never designed the human brain to operate through human performance, these good Christians are destined to fail and fall flat on their faces at some point. They can only carry the burden so long before they buckle under the tremendous weight of failure. Even then, unless someone teaches them what the Bible really says and they learn how God made the brain, these well-meaning people live in double bondage. They not only live in bondage to their sin of self-thinking, they live in bondage of false beliefs. They actually believe they are living in righteous suffering. Living in the suffering of our own cursed thinking is not the suffering God speaks about in the Bible. The suffering God describes is the hurt and pain his true focus-followers endure from the self-righteous so-called good Christians.

| *Uplifting* | *Discouraging* |
|---|---|
| ➢ | ➢ |
| ➢ | ➢ |
| ➢ | ➢ |

## *He Calls His Sheep by Name*

How can we be so sure that these self-righteous Christians are living in total denial and/or ignorance of God's master plan for our lives? Speaking for myself, I have been a self-righteous Christian my whole life. I only learned the truth about myself through studying God's Word and learning how God designed my brain. For most of my life, I thought my only option was to be self-righteous. Then God showed me that he never intended for me to be able to measure up to righteous living. He did not make my brain with that capacity. What a huge relief! God's purpose for the brain he made for me was nothing more than to give my sensory concentration to God. This way, he could use my brain to carry out his plan to save the world. I am simply his servant, his very happy servant. I am relieved that God clearly showed me that I am no longer stuck with the job of thinking for myself or acting on my own behalf.

Looking back, it now seems so obvious that trying to be my own leader was destined to fail from the start. And yet, both our culture and church promote leadership and individual achievement. It seems counterintuitive to desire being a servant and a follower. God's entire creation and his purpose for mankind was counterintuitive. From the very beginning of time, God's plan was for him to do all the thinking and to be the only voice in our heads. God wants us to focus and follow.

---

| *Uplifting* | *Discouraging* |
|---|---|
| ➢ | ➢ |
| ➢ | ➢ |
| ➢ | ➢ |

This plan is spelled out over and over again in the Bible. One of my favorite scriptures about focus is John 10:1-5:

> *"Let me set this before you as plainly as I can. If a person climbs over or through the fence of a sheep pen instead of going through the gate, you know he's up to no good—a sheep rustler! The shepherd walks right up to the gate. The gatekeeper opens the gate to him and the sheep recognize his voice. He calls his own sheep by name and leads them out. When he gets them all out, he leads them and they follow because they are familiar with his voice. They won't follow a stranger's voice but will scatter because they aren't used to the sound of it."*

Despite the simplicity of this message, verse 6 reminds us people had no clue what he was saying: Jesus told this simple story, but they had no idea what he was talking about.

In today's world, people think it is insane to say we are God's sheep and should follow his voice. I am sure a lot of people think I have gone off the deep end because I write about only wanting to follow God's voice and not my own. Public opinion was no different in Bible times:

> *This kind of talk caused another split in the Jewish ranks. A lot of them were saying, "He's crazy, a maniac—out of his head completely. Why bother listening to him?" But others weren't so sure: "These aren't the words of a crazy man. Can a 'maniac' open blind eyes?"* (John 10:19-21)

---

| *Uplifting* | *Discouraging* |
|---|---|
| ➢ | ➢ |
| ➢ | ➢ |
| ➢ | ➢ |

## *The Gift of Sensory Focus*

Throughout my life, my own thinking never led me to focus and follow God. I followed my own thinking, which was drilled into my brain by our culture and our church. I definitely knew how to think for myself and make independent decisions. I was taught to always stop and think about what I was about to say or what I was about to do. In essence, I was taught to be anxious. With only cursed thoughts to draw from, the outcome of my thinking was flawed and distorted toward the negative. Today, more than ever, we are taught how important our own thinking is. Many of my middle school clients show me elaborate behavioral worksheets designed by their teachers. The teachers have the students practice "thinking skills" designed to help students learn how to say and do the right things. The problem is that these highly technical self-reports focus exclusively on the thinking side of the brain. The teachers have not been taught how God made the brain. As a result, they are not able to show their students how to learn sensory focus skills so God can think and talk for these children.

The kids I work with are very open and even fascinated by how God made our brain and how he wants to be our voice in all we say and do. I work with one young student who struggles with sensory processing disorder. Certain sounds to him feel like screeching fingernails on a chalkboard. One of those sounds is coughing. When a classmate has a repetitive

| *Uplifting* | *Discouraging* |
|---|---|
| ➢ | ➢ |
| ➢ | ➢ |
| ➢ | ➢ |

cough, my client gets so frustrated that he forcefully holds his hand over the other child's mouth in his attempt to stop the coughing noise. Teachers and school counselors exhausted themselves attempting to teach classroom etiquette and thinking skills about the value of not hurting others. Despite their best logic and attempted training techniques, my client showed no improvement. This client did not have a violent personality nor did he intend to be mean or hurt anyone. But the noise of repetitive coughing really did send him to the moon. Teachers and parents were shocked at my suggestion: give this student the freedom to leave the room so he would not hear the coughing sounds.

Of course, leaving the sound of this noise behind corrected the problem for this client. He feels happy now because he has learned how to make irritating noises stop. This simple solution, which none of the school experts considered, was the secret to preventing this child from getting expelled from school. He learned the skill of sensory focus. The same thing can be said about all of us in today's world. How do we silence the noise of our own voice so we can be free to hear God's voice?

| *Uplifting* | *Discouraging* |
|---|---|
| ➢ | ➢ |
| ➢ | ➢ |
| ➢ | ➢ |

## *Our Bondage of Cursed Thinking*

Now that I have learned how God made the brain, it seems obvious to me why this child felt his only option was to stop the coughing noise. He felt defective because he would hold his hand over his classmate's mouth. He was told over and over again how wrong he was and needed to "stop" his bad behavior. He was made to feel something was wrong with him because he could not stop using his own willpower. Sadly, no one ever showed him "how" to stop. His teachers had not taught him how God made the brain, because they themselves had not learned. They were unaware that their student's sensory processing disorder made the sound of coughing unbearable. They did not know that God made the sensory side of our brain for the purpose of escaping the loud noise. No one gave him the option to leave the room. He was told to put up with the noise. He was not given the option of a way of escape.

Whether we recognize it or not, all of us are in the same predicament as this student. We are taught to try to live on our own willpower. We are taught right thoughts versus wrong thoughts. But no one has shown us how to live based on the correct thinking. More importantly, no one has shown us that only God has the correct thinking. No one has shown us how God made the brain, how to escape to God's thoughts, or how to live. Being born into the bondage of our own cursed thinking, we are trapped in our own mental prisons. Here is

| *Uplifting* | *Discouraging* |
|---|---|
| ➢ | ➢ |
| ➢ | ➢ |
| ➢ | ➢ |

how David described our cursed human condition in Psalm 107:10-16:

> *Some of you were locked in a dark cell,*
>   *cruelly confined behind bars,*
> *Punished for defying God's Word,*
>   *for turning your back on the High God's counsel—*
> *A hard sentence, and your hearts so heavy,*
>   *and not a soul in sight to help.*
> *Then you called out to God in your desperate condition;*
>   *he got you out in the nick of time.*
> *He led you out of your dark, dark cell,*
>   *broke open the jail and led you out.*
> *So thank God for his marvelous love,*
>   *for his miracle mercy to the children he loves;*
> *He shattered the heavy jailhouse doors,*
>   *he snapped the prison bars like matchsticks!*

---

| *Uplifting* | *Discouraging* |
|---|---|
| ➢ | ➢ |
| ➢ | ➢ |
| ➢ | ➢ |

## *Starting Over as Children*

Just as the solution that allowed this student to escape was simple yet profound, God's way of escape to him and his voice is just as simple and profound. Jesus told the disciples to be his little children who simply want to follow him as he tells us how to live:

> *At about the same time, the disciples came to Jesus asking, "Who gets the highest rank in God's kingdom?"*
>
> *For an answer Jesus called over a child, whom he stood in the middle of the room, and said, "I'm telling you, once and for all, that unless you return to square one and start over like children, you're not even going to get a look at the kingdom, let alone get in. Whoever becomes simple and elemental again, like this child, will rank high in God's kingdom. What's more, when you receive the childlike on my account, it's the same as receiving me.* (Matthew 18:1-5)

When children are very young, they live in the moment. They experience life only through their five senses of sight, sound, smell, touch and taste. They are at the total mercy of their caregiver to think for them and be their voice. They are also at the total mercy of their caregiver to protect them. For example, a young child sees a red, hot grill on the stovetop. They are drawn to touch it and badly burn their hand unless their caregiver protects them from reaching the

| *Uplifting* | *Discouraging* |
|---|---|
| ➤ | ➤ |
| ➤ | ➤ |
| ➤ | ➤ |

dangerous object. To the child, it is a hidden danger. Only their caregiver can keep them safe. The child feels safe in their caregiver's arms and will cry without their warm embrace.

Our culture and church have taught our children to "grow up." Children are taught to learn how to think for themselves and how to behave independently without having to be in the arms of their caregiver. As radical as his teaching may sound, God instructs us to return to being a child. He instructs us to live the sensory moment with him. God tells us to live in his arms under the protection of his safe embrace. These verses tell us, quite literally, to return to square one and start over like children. Without our five senses glued to him like a small child, we won't even get a glance at his kingdom, let alone get in. This statement is not meant as a threat by Jesus, he simply is saying sensory attention is the only way to live in the freedom of God's love.

I long for the day when parents, childcare workers, schools, coaches, and Sunday school teachers all show children how God made the brain. My counseling career began working with young children. They respond amazingly well to sensory focus therapy techniques. One young six-year-old girl was having great difficulty controlling her anger at her older brother who seemed to enjoy annoying her. Everyone tried to teach her not to kick her brother, without success. Of course, she saw herself as a bad little girl because of her behavioral outbursts. She hated the spankings her parents gave her for hitting her brother. Her little mind could not figure out why

---

| *Uplifting* | *Discouraging* |
|---|---|
| ➢ | ➢ |
| ➢ | ➢ |
| ➢ | ➢ |

she was not allowed to hit but her parents could. She felt so happy when she came up with the idea that helping her mommy cook would get her mind off her angry thoughts toward her brother. The smells in the kitchen captured her attention. She no longer felt the need to kick her brother.

| *Uplifting* | *Discouraging* |
|---|---|
| ➢ | ➢ |
| ➢ | ➢ |
| ➢ | ➢ |

| Uplifting | Discouraging |
|---|---|
| ➢ | ➢ |
| ➢ | ➢ |
| ➢ | ➢ |

## *Growing Up in Christ*

One critic of my focus and follow techniques (that I learned through study of the Bible and the brain) used an example from the Bible that talked about baby Christians growing up and becoming mature Christians. The critic used the following verses in Ephesians, which begins by stating that infants need to grow up:

> *No prolonged infancies among us, please. We'll not tolerate babes in the woods, small children who are an easy mark for impostors. God wants us to grow up, to know the whole truth and tell it in love—like Christ in everything. We take our lead from Christ, who is the source of everything we do. He keeps us in step with each other. His very breath and blood flow through us, nourishing us so that we will grow up healthy in God, robust in love.* (Ephesians 4:14-16)

I am so glad my critic pointed out these verses. Paul is indeed telling the Ephesians to grow up. Otherwise, infants are an easy target for imposters (false gods). The key question is "how" do we grow up. Our culture and church teach us to grow up by learning how to think, talk, and act responsibly. Sounds good, right? Yes, except for the fact that our own thinking is flawed, which can only result in flawed talk and flawed actions. Plus, we can't even correct our own thinking. No one can correct their thinking when it is flawed to begin with. In

| *Uplifting* | *Discouraging* |
|---|---|
| ➢ | ➢ |
| ➢ | ➢ |
| ➢ | ➢ |

our day and age where the definition of growing up is to become independent and to think for yourself and act responsibly, the biggest imposter is ourselves.

These verses tell us to grow up, not by becoming independent thinkers, but by keeping our total focus on Christ. That way we can take our lead from God, so he can be our sole voice and the source of everything we do. In fact, God is not only our voice when we give him our sensory focus, he becomes the very breath and blood that flow through us. The outcome is that we grow up healthy in God, and robust in love. God's description of how we grow up is just the opposite of what we have been taught all these years. Growing up in Christ means becoming increasingly more dependent on God, and not becoming an independent and responsible self-thinker with our own strong voice. Growing up in Christ is keeping our sensory focus on him more and more each day. As our sensory focus on God grows, our own imposter thoughts fade. Our voice becomes weaker, as God's voice in us becomes stronger, every day.

| *Uplifting* | *Discouraging* |
|---|---|
| ➢ | ➢ |
| ➢ | ➢ |
| ➢ | ➢ |

## *Our Own Twisted Thinking*

When God's voice grows stronger in our lives, we become more robust in his love. The link between God's strength and his robust love is straightforward, but our cursed thinking can disrupt this connection at any time. Even though God made each of us uniquely wonderful in his eyes, our own negative thoughts will condemn us without any warning. Without a conscious awareness of this dynamic, we all are easy targets to have our robust feelings of love hijacked by our own twisted thinking.

Our own thinking, words, and actions are abusive and neglectful to ourselves and others. The self-thinking of others is abusive and neglectful to us as well. I see these problems in my office multiple times a day: depression, anxiety, anger, physical abuse, sexual abuse, physical and emotional neglect, cutting and other forms of self-mutilation, and a host of addictions and other mental health disturbances. However, the most common theme clients bring to my office are their hateful thoughts about themselves. These thoughts block them from experiencing God's robust love. Without a continual sensory attachment to God so he can protect us, we are easy prey for the onslaught of nasty thoughts from our own cursed thinking and the cursed thinking of others.

The nasty thoughts to which we are exposed are endless. Our minds never run out of new negative thoughts to

| *Uplifting* | *Discouraging* |
|---|---|
| ➢ | ➢ |
| ➢ | ➢ |
| ➢ | ➢ |

label us. The following examples shared by my clients are just from the past week:

I am not thankful enough.

When God makes me happy, I feel guilty.

My thoughts are so depressive, they are painful.

My stomach is nauseous; my body feels frozen and petrified.

My thoughts are so bad, I am afraid to sleep because I will have dreams about them.

My thoughts are like a whirlwind, I am so terrified that I totally get it why people use drugs to escape or try to kill themselves.

These cursed-thought examples trace back to Adam and Eve eating from the tree of good and evil in the Garden of Eden. They chose to expose themselves to evil and we cannot protect ourselves from our fallen condition. We are all direct targets for being severely and repeatedly abused by our own thinking and the degenerative thinking of others. We have no clue that God gave us divine protection from such abuse. He made each of us as one of his miracle creations. Thankfully, God designed our brain so he can displace our own dreadful thoughts with his robust loving thoughts. How? Through the sensory attentiveness of our brain.

---

| *Uplifting* | *Discouraging* |
|---|---|
| ➢ | ➢ |
| ➢ | ➢ |
| ➢ | ➢ |

## *God's Grace is Enough*

Allowing God to fill us with his robust love can seem tricky at first. As fervently as many of us have begged God over the years to destroy our blemished thinking forever, God has a divine method to replace our awful thoughts with his uplifting thoughts. Paul describes God's method in his second letter to the people of Corinth:

> *If I had a mind to brag a little, I could probably do it without looking ridiculous, and I'd still be speaking plain truth all the way. But I'll spare you. I don't want anyone imagining me as anything other than the fool you'd encounter if you saw me on the street or heard me talk.*
>
> *Because of the extravagance of those revelations, and so I wouldn't get a big head, I was given the gift of a handicap to keep me in constant touch with my limitations. Satan's angel did his best to get me down; what he in fact did was push me to my knees. No danger then of walking around high and mighty! At first I didn't think of it as a gift, and begged God to remove it. Three times I did that, and then he told me,*
>
> > *My grace is enough; it's all you need.*
> > *My strength comes into its own in your weakness.*

---

| *Uplifting* | *Discouraging* |
|---|---|
| ➤ | ➤ |
| ➤ | ➤ |
| ➤ | ➤ |

*Once I heard that, I was glad to let it happen. I quit focusing on the handicap and began appreciating the gift. It was a case of Christ's strength moving in on my weakness. Now I take limitations in stride, and with good cheer, these limitations that cut me down to size—abuse, accidents, opposition, bad breaks. I just let Christ take over! And so the weaker I get, the stronger I become.* (2 Corinthians 12:6-12)

I have used these verses in several books I have written. Each time God gives me additional miracle thoughts about their meaning. In these verses, Paul described himself as any fool that you would hear talking on the street. Paul was acknowledging he is no different than any of us with our foolish thoughts. In fact, it is important for us to recognize our own cursed thoughts are foolish. Rather than God healing our foolish thoughts, he allows them to remain in us as a reminder to keep us in constant touch with their limitations. Satan tries to use our thoughts to destroy us. It is his way of trying to get us down and depressed. Like Paul, I know my own foolish thoughts have brought me to my knees many times. But, also like Paul, there is no longer any danger of me prancing around feeling high and mighty. I, too, begged God repeatedly to remove my miserable thinking.

However, as God has shown me how he made our brain, he has let me know that when my wicked thoughts resurface and make a guest appearance, it is actually a gift. How is that even remotely possible? Such is the supernatural

---

| *Uplifting* | *Discouraging* |
|---|---|
| ➢ | ➢ |
| ➢ | ➢ |
| ➢ | ➢ |

brilliance of God! He uses Satan's curse as a part of his plan to save us from destroying ourselves. God uses our curse—our broken spirit that comes from the battering we take from our own thinking—to invite us to escape to him with our sensory brain. God created our brain so we can use this escape to silence our thoughts. With our thoughts silenced and held captive through our sensory attachment to God, he pours out his thoughts in their place. He fills the thinking side of our brain with his thoughts instead of our own. To be specific: "My strength comes into its own in your weakness."

| *Uplifting* | *Discouraging* |
|---|---|
| ➢ | ➢ |
| ➢ | ➢ |
| ➢ | ➢ |

|  Uplifting | Discouraging |
| --- | --- |
| ➢ | ➢ |
| ➢ | ➢ |
| ➢ | ➢ |

## *Losing Control*

What a brilliant God to use our weakness to display his strength and fill us with his robust love. We can embrace his thoughts. We can hang on his every word. God's voice becomes our constant companion. We focus on God's voice instead of our own. We depend on him and not ourselves any longer. We have a whole new outlook on our own thoughts. Yes, our own terrible thoughts still have a place in our lives, but we no longer feel condemned by them. We thank God for our own distasteful thoughts. They are clear, constant reminders and a catalyst for us to run from them into the arms of God. We take them in stride. They no longer have any power to bring us down. The super power of God's thoughts keeps us happy, feeling his robust love, and in "good cheer." Previously, our own thoughts took us to abuse, accidents, opposition, and bad breaks. Now they take us to Christ. He takes over! The more we see our own thoughts as weak, the stronger we become in God's robust love.

When I began to practice sensory focus on a constant basis, I felt like I was flying by the seat of my pants. I felt like I was losing my mind. I felt like I was losing control. Truth be told, I was losing the thinking side of my brain; I was losing control. As I practiced making the continual, conscious choice to attach my five senses to God, I lost control of my thought life. With my sensory focus on God, he could take control of my thought life. I let God do all the thinking, which meant he

| *Uplifting* | *Discouraging* |
|---|---|
| ➢ | ➢ |
| ➢ | ➢ |
| ➢ | ➢ |

also took over my voice and my actions. Through sensory closeness with God, he provides his thoughts, words, and actions to live by. I became his messenger, simply a servant. I became a slave to Christ; yet, I felt free for the first time in my life. Yes, God did set me free. He set me free from the tyranny of my own thoughts. He set me free from myself.

My favorite example of God setting me free from the tyranny of my own thoughts is reading the Bible and sharing the thoughts he gives me through writing this and other books. I feel completely freed from worrisome thoughts about my past or my future. It's a wonderful feeling to be on the receiving end of God giving me the exact words to write. What a fascinating journey. What a way. The only way. Letting God fill us with his robust love.

| *Uplifting* | *Discouraging* |
|---|---|
| ➤ | ➤ |
| ➤ | ➤ |
| ➤ | ➤ |

## *The Power of Love*

What does it feel like to be filled with God's robust love? It is an incredible feeling, unmatched by any feeling that I have ever experienced before in my life! For me, it is the ultimate feeling of a natural high, or should I say, a supernatural high! It is a high I feel even during grueling circumstances. I feel God's robust love when I am hurting or exhausted, either physically or emotionally. His feeling of love always surprises me at the most unexpected times. When I feel lonely and uncared-for by others, God always lifts me up with his wonderful love.

In the early stages of my sensory focus on God, I felt insecure in his love like I had always felt in human love. I was fearful his love would be snatched away from me at any moment. To my great surprise, this feeling of God's robust love does not ever leave or forsake me. In fact, just the opposite has occurred. His love keeps lifting me higher and higher and then keeps me standing on that higher ground. I know, God is flooding my mind with so many songs that I sang over the years. Like the popular rhythm and blues song by Jackie Wilson from 1967, "(Your Love Keeps Lifting Me) Higher and Higher" (Rita Coolidge covered the song ten years later):

| *Uplifting* | *Discouraging* |
|---|---|
| ➢ | ➢ |
| ➢ | ➢ |
| ➢ | ➢ |

> Your love keeps liftin' me higher
> Than I've ever been lifted before
> So keep it up, quench my desire
> And I'll be at your side forevermore

Or, the hymn "I'm Pressing on the Upward Way [Higher Ground]" by Johnson Oatman, Jr., written in 1898:

> I'm pressing on the upward way,
> New heights I'm gaining every day;
> Still praying as I'm onward bound,
> "Lord, plant my feet on higher ground."
>
> > Lord, lift me up and let me stand,
> > By faith, on Heaven's tableland,
> > A higher plane than I have found;
> > Lord, plant my feet on higher ground.

There are also beautiful verses in the Bible that describe God's bountiful love in us. And by the way, the so-called experts that keep trying to say that "love is not a feeling" need many lessons from the Bible and the brain. God clearly made his love to be a matchless feeling, a feeling we never experience until we experience God in the moment with our five senses. The feeling of his supernatural love releases way more pleasure chemicals in our body than any natural or chemical high.

Not surprisingly, with God as the master neuroscientist, our brain is the most important organ for love.

---

| *Uplifting* | *Discouraging* |
|---|---|
| ➢ | ➢ |
| ➢ | ➢ |
| ➢ | ➢ |

Dr. Helen Fisher, a biological anthropologist, has spent her academic life trying to figure out what's going on in the brains of those who are in the throes of passionate, romantic love. Dr. Fisher scanned the brains of young lovers and published this on BrainHQ.com[9]:

> ...[W]hen they're focusing on the object of their affection, a whole host of brain parts start lighting up.
> ...[T]he brain areas associated with dopamine and norepinephrine production light up. Both are brain chemicals associated with pleasurable activities and excitement.

Dr. Fisher also gave a TedTalk[10] about how the brain reacts when it's in love. Giving our sensory focus to God, the producer of his love in our lives, is all we have to do to start lighting up our brain for the chemicals associated with pleasurable activities and excitement to be released. We can focus on other things that also release pleasure chemicals, but nothing can compare to God's love.

| *Uplifting* | *Discouraging* |
|---|---|
| ➢ | ➢ |
| ➢ | ➢ |
| ➢ | ➢ |

|   Uplifting    |   Discouraging   |
| --- | --- |
| ➢ | ➢ |
| ➢ | ➢ |
| ➢ | ➢ |

## *Hard Times*

When faced with hard times, how do we respond? The solution is in living life on God's terms:

*So, what do you think? With God on our side like this, how can we lose? If God didn't hesitate to put everything on the line for us, embracing our condition and exposing himself to the worst by sending his own Son, is there anything else he wouldn't gladly and freely do for us? And who would dare tangle with God by messing with one of God's chosen? Who would dare even to point a finger? The One who died for us—who was raised to life for us!—is in the presence of God at this very moment sticking up for us. Do you think anyone is going to be able to drive a wedge between us and Christ's love for us? There is no way! Not trouble, not hard times, not hatred, not hunger, not homelessness, not bullying threats, not backstabbing, not even the worst sins listed in Scripture:*

*They kill us in cold blood because they hate you. We're sitting ducks; they pick us off one by one.*

*None of this fazes us because Jesus loves us. I'm absolutely convinced that nothing—nothing living or dead, angelic or demonic, today or tomorrow, high or low, thinkable or unthinkable—absolutely nothing can get between us and God's love because of the way that Jesus our Master has embraced us.* (Romans 8:34-39)

| *Uplifting* | *Discouraging* |
|---|---|
| ➤ | ➤ |
| ➤ | ➤ |
| ➤ | ➤ |

All of us have endured some measure of hard times. And some people have even faced the possibility of being killed in cold blood. I knew someone who went through the Killing Fields during the communist Khmer Rouge regime in Cambodia. This person recalled their family, including the children, throwing themselves on a pile of dead bodies as a disguise to appear they were already dead. These scriptures highlight the depth of Christ's love being so captivating that no measure of hard times can pull our sensory focus away from his love. God designed the sensory side of our brain to have the incredible capacity to be glued to him and his love. Full-on sensory attachment to God is the only means for God's robust love to penetrate our hearts to the degree of keeping our eyes on him no matter how traumatic our situation is.

I worked in residential addiction treatment programs for nearly 20 years. Every day I witnessed the strong love link between clients and their addictions. These addicts would leave their jobs, their schools, and even their loved ones to give their full sensory attention to alcohol and drugs. Their sensory attention was glued to their addiction. The only wedge that can separate the addict from their addiction is God's love. Only God's love is powerful enough to replace earthly addiction with heavenly addiction, and sensory devotion to God is the only way to open the door to the power of his love in our lives.

How do we know God's love has taken over our lives? Frequently, others notice before we notice ourselves. Remember, we are no longer selfish and stuck on self-

| *Uplifting* | *Discouraging* |
|---|---|
| ➤ | ➤ |
| ➤ | ➤ |
| ➤ | ➤ |

observation. We simply give God our sensory attention and follow him. We follow his voice and do what he tells us. When I give this simple answer to my clients they look at me as if I am asking them to do the impossible. My response to their doubt is always the same. Many of us have devoted our sensory attention to various addictions. We have listened to our addiction, heard the voice of our addiction loud and clear, and followed our addiction to the ends of the earth. God designed our brains so we could closely follow him anywhere he leads us. God wants us to follow him in heavenly addiction rather than spending another day devoted to our earthly addictions. Following God brings us supernatural love rather than earthly destruction.

| *Uplifting* | *Discouraging* |
|---|---|
| ➤ | ➤ |
| ➤ | ➤ |
| ➤ | ➤ |

| Uplifting | Discouraging |
|---|---|
| ➢ | ➢ |
| ➢ | ➢ |
| ➢ | ➢ |

# God's Love, Delivered Fresh Daily

How does God deliver his robust love? God delivers his love in infinite ways. It is important to highlight the word "deliver." Growing up on a rural dairy farm in central Pennsylvania, we were accustomed to delivery men and their trucks. We had a milk man, a bakery man, a pretzel and chips man, a tractor repair man; the list was endless. God, as a delivery man, brings us something no one else can: the feeling of love. Most would argue that we humans generate the feeling of love from inside ourselves. Not so! God did not design our brain expecting us to come up with the feeling of love on our own.

God is the source of all love. As humans, we are only capable of hate. Our hatred began when Adam and Eve listened to the creator of hatred and ate from the tree of good and evil. Since that time, humans have been able to spread only hatred around the world. Only when we recognize our inability to deliver love ourselves are we able to call on God to deliver his incredible love. He has an endless supply to deliver. And God never takes a holiday!

I was a witness to one of God's great love deliveries at a very unusual location yesterday: the criminal court in Howard County, Maryland. I was testifying as an expert witness in a case involving a prisoner with four DUI's who was facing a year of jail time for his recurring offenses. The

| *Uplifting* | *Discouraging* |
|---|---|
| ➤ | ➤ |
| ➤ | ➤ |
| ➤ | ➤ |

presiding judge scolded him for not learning his lesson after his third DUI when the police tried to shoot him for attempting to escape. Of course, he was drunk at the time, so an aversive memory to drink again did not register in his mind. However, the prisoner told the judge that he will never drink again because of the aversive memory of his one-year-old son not being able to see his daddy in jail. A powerful, loving memory did register in his brain when mommy brought his baby to the visitor's window at the jail. Daddy saw his son put his tiny hand on the glass hoping to touch his daddy. Daddy thanked God for this memory. It was a tender feeling of God's love through his infant son.

God has endless ways of delivering his love. He gives us thoughts and gestures that warm our hearts with thankfulness and love. He delivers smells and sounds and tastes and sights and touch that fill us with his goodness. The only requirement is for us to have our five senses attentive to God. The problem, from my personal and professional experience, is sensory focus. This was the biggest secret of all in our relationship with God, until we learned his design for our brain. When God showed me the power of sensory focus, it transformed my life and my relationship with him. God delivers uplifting thoughts directly to my brain that make me feel thankful and loving. When we allow God to fill our minds with thankful and loving thoughts, this passion gives us an aversion to sin, as opposed to our own thoughts, which remain passionate toward sin.

| *Uplifting* | *Discouraging* |
|---|---|
| ➢ | ➢ |
| ➢ | ➢ |
| ➢ | ➢ |

## *Be Alert!*

Under whose authority can I possibly say that God's thoughts deliver love while our own thoughts deliver condemnation? It is important that the ultimate authority on this be God, and not my own thoughts. This is true especially in a modern-day culture and church that worship great speakers and writers. In today's culture, mega-churches fill auditoriums and stadiums with tens of thousands of people. They can also attract millions of television and internet followers. Almost without exception, these famous speakers and writers are clueless about how God made the brain. They use eloquent words and give instructions that are meaningless and sometimes terribly harmful. Their teaching is all too often the opposite of what God teaches. Everything I write must be confirmed by what God says in his Word and be in line with how he made the brain.

For starters, God makes a sharp and very clear distinction between his thoughts and man's thoughts. In fact, he makes such a radical contrast that there is no argument distinguishing God's voice and our voice. Any such argument is merely a concoction of man's faulty thinking. In Paul's letter to the Romans, he says we all start out as sinners. Paul then admonishes them that scripture leaves no doubt about the condition of man's thinking:

| *Uplifting* | *Discouraging* |
|---|---|
| ➢ | ➢ |
| ➢ | ➢ |
| ➢ | ➢ |

*There's nobody living right, not even one,*
  *nobody who knows the score, nobody alert for God.*
*They've all taken the wrong turn;*
  *they've all wandered down blind alleys.*
*No one's living right;*
  *I can't find a single one.*
*Their throats are gaping graves,*
  *their tongues slick as mudslides.*
*Every word they speak is tinged with poison.*
  *They open their mouths and pollute the air.*
*They race for the honor of sinner-of-the-year,*
  *litter the land with heartbreak and ruin,*
*Don't know the first thing about living with others.*
  *They never give God the time of day.*
(Romans 3:10-16)

Whew! Those verses set me straight every time I read them. Not one of us has been "alert" to God. What is the mechanism in the brain God designed for us that makes us alert? The sensory side of the brain that receives incoming stimuli is the part of the brain God installed in us to be alert: sensory alert! Because of our lack of sensory attention to God, we all wander down blind alleys. Our tongues are slick as mudslides. We speak where every word is poison. Not just some of our thinking is tainted. All our thoughts need to be thrown out as trash. Our thoughts cannot be salvaged. Our thoughts cannot be repaired. They all need to be replaced with God's thoughts, with God's voice.

---

| *Uplifting* | *Discouraging* |
|---|---|
| ➢ | ➢ |
| ➢ | ➢ |
| ➢ | ➢ |

## *Snowdrifts of Thoughts*

Sensory alertness to God is the exact path for total replacement of our thoughts with God's thoughts. The word "total" means we stay in continual prayer with God. Continual prayer does not mean constant traditional prayers to God. It means the constant, conscious choice to be fully alert to him with our five senses. Sensory alertness is not a quality highlighted in the modern-day secular and church culture. Thinking and reasoning are highlighted to the extreme. Mankind seems to be obsessively driven to overcome it's cursed thinking on its own. It is very predictable that cursed thinking would be obsessed with itself. Sad but true, this obsession is what separates us from God's love. When I was growing up on the dairy farm in Pennsylvania, we had lots of snow every winter. Huge snowdrifts would prevent the delivery trucks from getting to our farm. Our own thinking causes huge snowdrifts in our brain that prevent God from delivering his love to our doorstep. What a life-giving delivery we are missing!

As much as our own thinking ruins our lives, God's thinking can deliver a total rescue because of his abundant love. He holds nothing back. God loves us so much that he gave his only son to die on the cross. Christ's death and resurrection were the centerpiece of God's plan to replace our cursed thinking with his divine thinking in our lives. Only this selfless display of God's love could penetrate and destroy the

| *Uplifting* | *Discouraging* |
|---|---|
| ➤ | ➤ |
| ➤ | ➤ |
| ➤ | ➤ |

curse. That is how strong the curse of our own thinking is. The law was not able to break the curse. Only God's love was strong enough. Now that I learned how God made our brain, I understand why and how only his love can rescue us from our own thinking. God designed our brain so our sensory entrance receives his love when we cast our five senses on him. God's love is so powerful that his divine outpouring totally captivates our senses. Our sensor brain is so mesmerized that our cursed thoughts are silenced. The curse has finally been broken. Now, all we must do is to keep our five senses on God so we can continually be filled with his love. Being filled with his love is the one and only way to keep our thoughts silenced:

> *God is love. When we take up permanent residence in a life of love, we live in God and God lives in us. This way, love has the run of the house, becomes at home and mature in us, so that we're free of worry on Judgment Day—our standing in the world is identical with Christ's. There is no room in love for fear. Well-formed love banishes fear. Since fear is crippling, a fearful life— fear of death, fear of judgment—is one not yet fully formed in love.*
>
> *We, though, are going to love—love and be loved. First we were loved, now we love. He loved us first.* (1 John 4:17-19)

---

*Uplifting*                              *Discouraging*

➤                                        ➤

➤                                        ➤

➤                                        ➤

# The Extravagant Dimensions of God's Love

The source of our fear is our thoughts. The source of our thoughts is Satan. This double link began in the Garden of Eden when Adam and Eve listened to Satan's voice and ate from the tree of good and evil. Partaking of the fruit exposed them to evil—Satan's evil voice. This direct exposure to his voice caused man to fear. Mankind has been crippled by fear ever since and doomed to follow Satan's voice. Unless, of course, humans make the simple choice to let God become their voice instead of Satan. Unfortunately, many of us try to overcome Satan on our own. God did not construct our brain with this capability. Remember, it all starts with God loving us first. He constructed our brain to receive his love through sensory focus on him. This focus is how God's love can take up residence in us. In fact, our sensory devotion to God gives his love run of the house. Well-formed sensory focus allows God's love to banish fear from our lives. God's love is the only way for us to be free from our own worrisome thoughts. Otherwise, we live a fearful life. Our brain is not capable of forming love on its own. God made our brains to be a passage for his love to enter us, dwell in us, and radiate through us to others. Now that I have learned how God made our brain, I marvel that God would want me (and you) to be the dwelling place and home for his love:

| *Uplifting* | *Discouraging* |
|---|---|
| ➢ | ➢ |
| ➢ | ➢ |
| ➢ | ➢ |

# The Bible and the Brain 195

> *My response is to get down on my knees before the Father, this magnificent Father who parcels out all heaven and earth. I ask him to strengthen you by his Spirit—not a brute strength but a glorious inner strength—that Christ will live in you as you open the door and invite him in. And I ask him that with both feet planted firmly on love, you'll be able to take in with all followers of Jesus the extravagant dimensions of Christ's love. Reach out and experience the breadth! Test its length! Plumb the depths! Rise to the heights! Live full lives, full in the fullness of God.* (Ephesians 3:14-19)

When we keep our five senses firmly focused on God, we open our door to take in the extravagant dimensions of God's love. His love goes on full display in us as we live in the sensory moment with God. We reach out and experience its breadth, we test its length, we plumb its depth, and rise to its heights. In other words, God uses me, the same miserable person who was crippled by fear for most of his life, to showcase his love.

---

*Uplifting*                                  *Discouraging*

➤                                            ➤


➤                                            ➤


➤                                            ➤

## *Flip the Switch to God*

The experience of God's love in and through me is so extravagant that I am left with no doubts—it is God in me and not my own doing. My own crippled self still makes plenty of guest appearances to remind me of the immeasurable distance between God's uplifting thoughts and my pathetic ones. God made my brain with a distinct sensory memory of my awful thought life. God uses my memory to remind me to sprint back to his thoughts when mine make an ugly, and predictable, reappearance. Fortunately, the mechanism in our brain God created to sprint back to his thoughts is fast-acting. In fact, this sensory mechanism can keep us from being swallowed up by our own self-destructive thinking. God designed our brain to be able to quickly flip from our reappearing thoughts to his thoughts through the five rhythmic senses he created at the welcome center of our brain. We simply choose to flip the switch from our nasty thoughts to the rhythms of our five senses. The flip welcomes his loving thoughts to pour into us rather than being trapped in our own defective thinking. The longer I live in sensory focus on God, the more he shows me the vast chasm between my thoughts and his thoughts. I was taught to pride myself in thinking for myself. Today, I am continually thankful that God gave me a way of escape from the mental prison of my own thinking. I feel free at last, simply to be happy with my brain immersed in God's love.

---

| *Uplifting* | *Discouraging* |
|---|---|
| ➢ | ➢ |
| ➢ | ➢ |
| ➢ | ➢ |

Whenever I need a refresher about my freedom in God's generous love, I read one of David's many writings in the Psalms:

*Generous in love—God, give grace!*
  *Huge in mercy—wipe out my bad record.*
*Scrub away my guilt,*
  *soak out my sins in your laundry.*
*I know how bad I've been;*
  *my sins are staring me down.*

*You're the One I've violated, and you've seen*
  *it all, seen the full extent of my evil.*
*You have all the facts before you;*
  *whatever you decide about me is fair.*
*I've been out of step with you for a long time,*
  *in the wrong since before I was born.*
*What you're after is truth from the inside out.*
  *Enter me, then; conceive a new, true life.*

*Soak me in your laundry and I'll come out clean,*
  *scrub me and I'll have a snow-white life.*
*Tune me in to foot-tapping songs,*
  *set these once-broken bones to dancing.*
*Don't look too close for blemishes,*
  *give me a clean bill of health.*
*God, make a fresh start in me,*
  *shape a Genesis week from the chaos of my life.*
(Psalm 51:1-10)

---

| *Uplifting* | *Discouraging* |
|---|---|
| ➢ | ➢ |
| ➢ | ➢ |
| ➢ | ➢ |

David wrote these verses after he had an affair with Bathsheba and killed her husband. If God can set David's feet to dancing, I know God can fill me with his love when I give my rhythmic sensory attention to him. As David lamented, this close sensory attachment to God always silences my haunting thoughts about how bad my record has been, since before I was born.

| *Uplifting* | *Discouraging* |
|---|---|
| ➢ | ➢ |
| ➢ | ➢ |
| ➢ | ➢ |

|  Uplifting  |  Discouraging  |
| --- | --- |
| ➢ | ➢ |
| ➢ | ➢ |
| ➢ | ➢ |

## *The Wind in My Sails*

In my human imagination, I simply cannot embrace why God would want to love me after my lifetime of being out of step with him. Yet, if God pulled it off in David's life, he can consummate his miraculous supernatural love in all our lives. How does God keep us from going back to our own thinking and our old life? Here is how God accomplished this feat in David's life and put a "fresh wind in his sails" following David's sinful behavior with Bathsheba:

> *Don't throw me out with the trash,*
>   *or fail to breathe holiness in me.*
> *Bring me back from gray exile,*
>   *put a fresh wind in my sails!*
> *Give me a job teaching rebels your ways*
>   *so the lost can find their way home.*
> *Commute my death sentence, God, my salvation God,*
>   *and I'll sing anthems to your life-giving ways.*
> *Unbutton my lips, dear God;*
>   *I'll let loose with your praise.* (Psalm 51:11-15)

These verses very clearly describe God's plan for David to stay in close sensory communion with God following the horrific behaviors that brought David to the end of himself. God breathed holiness into David and a put fresh wind in his sails by giving him a job—teaching rebels his ways. Even though we deserve a death sentence, God grants us a full

---

| *Uplifting* | *Discouraging* |
|---|---|
| ➤ | ➤ |
| ➤ | ➤ |
| ➤ | ➤ |

pardon and puts us to work sharing with others the miracles he accomplished in our lives.

While God does all this in our lives, we do play a part. From these verses in Psalm 51, we learn that our part is to sing anthems to his life-giving ways. As God unbuttons our lips, we let loose with his praise. In other words, our part is rhythmic sensory participation so God can spread his powerful love through us. Since I cannot sing, my rhythmic sensory participation includes writing, speaking, and counseling. For example, my writing is rhythmic as I type one letter at a time on my iPhone. As absurd as that sounds, God delivers the words to me at about the same speed as I type. Amazingly, I feel at complete rest when I engage in this writing and experience total freedom from my old, annoying thoughts. I love God's thoughts and his words over my own. God makes me feel incredibly special to him as I give him my sensory attachment through my writing. I am so grateful not to have to put up with my old thoughts or voice anymore.

| *Uplifting* | *Discouraging* |
|---|---|
| ➢ | ➢ |
| ➢ | ➢ |
| ➢ | ➢ |

## *Hitting Bottom*

How did I come to the place in my life where I was happy to be free from my old sinful self and bad record? It most certainly was not because I came up with the bright idea to follow God on my own. Like all of us, I am always a work in progress. God sanctifies me more and more every day as I devote my sensory self to him. David also had the same answer to this "how" question in Psalm 51:16-17:

> *Going through the motions doesn't please you,*
>   *a flawless performance is nothing to you.*
> *I learned God-worship*
>   *when my pride was shattered.*
> *Heart-shattered lives ready for love*
>   *don't for a moment escape God's notice.*

One of my favorite ways to devote my sensory self to God is through frequent reading of his Word and writing down the thoughts and words that God shares with me during these sensory moments. The above verses are a prime example of how God loves on me when I give him my sensory attention through reading and writing. I cannot say I had never read these verses before; but, as I read them now, I marvel at their meaning. For most of my life, I just went through the motions. I lived in the thinking side of my brain—my own thinking. Many of us have been taught that is the Christian way to live. However, the Bible does not teach the thinking way of living.

| *Uplifting* | *Discouraging* |
|---|---|
| ➢ | ➢ |
| ➢ | ➢ |
| ➢ | ➢ |

Living in the moment with our senses tuned in and alert to God is the way to live. That is the only way to not just go through the motions. When we live primarily in the self-thinking mode we are just going through the motions, without engaging our five senses.

Just going through the motions by dwelling on our own thoughts is what pride is all about. Pride is a certainty when we are self-thinkers. Self-thinking also leads us toward a heart-shattered life. Just going through the motions ensures our needs to love and to be loved never get fulfilled. We have only our cursed thoughts and pride as our companions. Misery and heartbreak are guaranteed outcomes. That is a tragic way to live.

That was the story of my life until I learned how God made the brain and I began to read his Word every chance I got. Directing the attention of my five senses to God turned off my self-thinking brain, tuned my attention into God's thoughts and words, and made me ready for love. God is so loving that his heart breaks every time our heart is broken. God knows that we all live with a broken heart until we discover how to tune into his love. God does not withhold his love from anyone. We simply do not receive his love until we run to him with all our senses.

---

| *Uplifting* | *Discouraging* |
|---|---|
| ➤ | ➤ |
| ➤ | ➤ |
| ➤ | ➤ |

## *Our Backs Turned to God*

When we run to God and tune into him with our five senses, our brain soaks up the immeasurable love that God wants to pour into us. The sensory side of our brain is the soaking-in entrance for God's love:

> *In alert expectancy such as this, we're never left feeling shortchanged. Quite the contrary—we can't round up enough containers to hold everything God generously pours into our lives through the Holy Spirit!* (Romans 5:5)

The scriptures are consistently clear that sensory alertness is the only way to receive and experience God's love. Paul is telling the Romans that sensory alertness is the secret to hearing God's voice through the Holy Spirit. At this point in my life, nothing matches the love I experience deep inside me when God talks to me. I will never be able to fully grasp why such a majestic God would take the time to give me constant, loving attention as if I am his only child. The beauty of God and his love is he desires to give every one of us this constant, loving attention.

I feel this loving attention every time I read the Bible with sensory fervor—without a single distraction for any of my senses. The apostle Paul describes God's love with great passion. He tells how we were brought over to God's side without sensory distractions by our own rebellious thoughts:

| *Uplifting* | *Discouraging* |
|---|---|
| ➢ | ➢ |
| ➢ | ➢ |
| ➢ | ➢ |

*You yourselves are a case study of what he does. At one time you all had your backs turned to God, thinking rebellious thoughts of him, giving him trouble every chance you got. But now, by giving himself completely at the Cross, actually dying for you, Christ brought you over to God's side and put your lives together, whole and holy in his presence. You don't walk away from a gift like that! You stay grounded and steady in that bond of trust, constantly tuned in to the Message, careful not to be distracted or diverted. There is no other Message—just this one. Every creature under heaven gets this same Message. I, Paul, am a messenger of this Message.* (Colossians 1:21-23)

Paul does not mince words. It is not possible to receive God's love when we have our backs turned to him. With our backs turned, we are totally at the mercy of our brain thinking rebellious thoughts about him. We did not turn around on our own so-called wise thoughts. Christ turned us around and brought us over to God's side by giving himself completely at the Cross, and actually dying for us. Now that Christ turned us around, we stay tuned-in to his matchless love of being willing to suffer a cruel death on the cross just to capture our sensory attention. By staying focused on his death and resurrection, we stay grounded and steady through constantly being tuned into this Message with our five senses, careful not to be distracted or diverted.

---

*Uplifting*                              *Discouraging*

➢                                        ➢

➢                                        ➢

➢                                        ➢

## *Going Through Hard Times*

The sole reason I founded FocusChoice Therapy, the first Christian therapy model, was to support Paul as "a messenger of this Message." With any client I see or book that I write, my one desire is that we all become messengers of this Message. Being a messenger is a fundamental way to have an intense experience of God's love. It is a vital way for God to increase our passion to keep our five senses on God. It is the same principle that Alcoholics Anonymous follows: "Give it away to keep it." Paul, the original messenger of this Message, makes many connections between receiving God's love and then sharing it with others:

> *He comes alongside us when we go through hard times, and before you know it, he brings us alongside someone else who is going through hard times so that we can be there for that person just as God was there for us.* (2 Corinthians 1:4)

I was going through very hard times when God came alongside me. Without a doubt, God has always been patiently waiting by my side to rescue me from hard times. I simply did not tune my senses toward God until I hit a sensory rock bottom. At that point I was so desperate that I turned my senses to him. This simple choice allowed God to pour his love into me. Very quickly, as God came alongside me, I began to write so I could come alongside others through my writing. This

| *Uplifting* | *Discouraging* |
|---|---|
| ➢ | ➢ |
| ➢ | ➢ |
| ➢ | ➢ |

writing gave birth to FocusChoice Therapy. I have not stopped writing since God rescued me. Writing has become so meaningful to me as a powerful way to stay in close sensory connection with God and to share his Message of love with others.

John wrote three letters basically telling us how to love the right way by dealing with God the right way. In this passage, John encourages all of us to continue this love relationship:

> *My beloved friends, let us continue to love each other since love comes from God. Everyone who loves is born of God and experiences a relationship with God. The person who refuses to love doesn't know the first thing about God, because God is love—so you can't know him if you don't love. This is how God showed his love for us: God sent his only Son into the world so we might live through him. This is the kind of love we are talking about—not that we once upon a time loved God, but that he loved us and sent his Son as a sacrifice to clear away our sins and the damage they've done to our relationship with God.* (1 John 4:7-10)

| *Uplifting* | *Discouraging* |
|---|---|
| ➢ | ➢ |
| ➢ | ➢ |
| ➢ | ➢ |

## *Once Upon a Time*

The apostle Paul is a great example of how God's love can totally transform someone, of how God uses our brain to do a miraculous work in us. Before God transformed Paul, his name was Saul. Saul was full of hate towards those who believed Jesus was the Christ, and was part of a mob who stoned Stephen to death:

> *At that point they went wild, a rioting mob of catcalls and whistles and invective. But Stephen, full of the Holy Spirit, hardly noticed—he only had eyes for God, whom he saw in all his glory with Jesus standing at his side. He said, "Oh! I see heaven wide open and the Son of Man standing at God's side!"*
>
> *Yelling and hissing, the mob drowned him out. Now in full stampede, they dragged him out of town and pelted him with rocks. The ringleaders took off their coats and asked a young man named Saul to watch them.*
>
> *As the rocks rained down, Stephen prayed, "Master Jesus, take my life." Then he knelt down, praying loud enough for everyone to hear, "Master, don't blame them for this sin"—his last words. Then he died.* (Acts 7:54-60)

It is very difficult to imagine that the same man who congratulated the killers of Stephen became Paul. A man once

| *Uplifting* | *Discouraging* |
|---|---|
| ➤ | ➤ |
| ➤ | ➤ |
| ➤ | ➤ |

consumed with hate became a man overflowing with love and compassion. This radical change could only be the work of God. God could do this work in Paul because he made the human brain to be his instrument of transformation. God made our brain to be receptive and deeply impacted by his supernatural interventions. God intervened in Saul's life on the road to Damascus:

> *All this time Saul was breathing down the necks of the Master's disciples, out for the kill. He went to the Chief Priest and got arrest warrants to take to the meeting places in Damascus so that if he found anyone there belonging to the Way, whether men or women, he could arrest them and bring them to Jerusalem.*
>
> *He set off. When he got to the outskirts of Damascus, he was suddenly dazed by a blinding flash of light. As he fell to the ground, he heard a voice: "Saul, Saul, why are you out to get me?"*
>
> *He said, "Who are you, Master?"*
>
> *"I am Jesus, the One you're hunting down. I want you to get up and enter the city. In the city you'll be told what to do next."* (Acts 9:1-6)

---

*Uplifting*                                *Discouraging*

➢                            ➢

➢                            ➢

➢                            ➢

## *God Made Our Mind to See*

I am fascinated how God made our brain. He made it so different from how we think he made it. No surprise there. By our very nature, our thinking is distorted, so our idea of how God made our brain is wrong. God did not make our brain for us to dwell on our thinking side and think for ourselves. He made our brain to be able to see—to see with our five senses. Thankfully, as the creator of all things, God can display his creation in a sensational way. God used a shocking display to get Saul's attention as he traveled to Damascus. God put Saul in a daze with blinding light. Then, as Saul fell to the ground, God stunned Saul with the sound of his voice. He asked Saul why he was out to get God. Saul did not know who the voice belonged to, but he instantly knew that the voice belonged to a Master. A Master who had control over his mind, control over his brain. God left no doubt he had a voice which can capture our attention. God left no doubt his design for our brain is for God to be at the control tower of our thinking side.

To ensure he left no doubt in Saul's mind about his supernatural authority, God made Saul blind:

> *His companions stood there dumbstruck—they could hear the sound, but couldn't see anyone—while Saul, picking himself up off the ground, found himself stone-blind. They had to take him by the hand and lead him into Damascus. He continued blind for three days. He ate nothing, drank nothing.* (Acts 9:7-9)

| *Uplifting* | *Discouraging* |
|---|---|
| ➢ | ➢ |
| ➢ | ➢ |
| ➢ | ➢ |

God's method of capturing our attention through the sensory side of our brain and being the commander and voice through our thinking side simply blows my mind every time I read the Bible. In this case, God gave Saul a crash course in sensory dependency on the Master. Although it heightened his other senses, being blind required Saul to let himself be led by the hand.

Being blind and dependent on others was God's way of delivering Saul from a life of killing followers of the Message. Being made blind was just a part of God's sensory work in Saul. God did not restrict his work to eyesight. Saul also did not eat or drink anything. Then God gave Saul a dream, and spoke to Ananias in a vision:

> *"Get up and go over to Straight Avenue. Ask at the house of Judas for a man from Tarsus. His name is Saul. He's there praying. He has just had a dream in which he saw a man named Ananius enter the house and lay hands on him so he could see again."* (Acts 9:11-12)

Saul was "born again," into to a radical life of being God's messenger—as Paul—and leading the spiritually blind to Jesus.

---

| *Uplifting* | *Discouraging* |
|---|---|
| ➢ | ➢ |
| ➢ | ➢ |
| ➢ | ➢ |

## *Don't Argue with God*

While the centerpiece of the verses in Acts 9 was about God's conversion of Saul to Paul through his sensory work, God was simultaneously doing his sensory work in Ananias. God used a vision to tell Ananias to go to where Saul was staying at the house of Judas. As he did with Saul, God had to use his sensory power to overcome the doubting protests of Ananias's thinking:

> *Ananias protested, "Master, you can't be serious. Everybody's talking about this man and the terrible things he's been doing, his reign of terror against your people in Jerusalem! And now he's shown up here with papers from the Chief Priest that give him license to do the same to us."*
>
> *But the Master said, "Don't argue. Go! I have picked him as my personal representative to non-Jews and kings and Jews."* (Acts 9:13-15)

In many situations in our own lives, our own thinking does appear to be rational. Ananias certainly had valid concerns about Saul's terrible actions against God's people. Certainly no human argument could oppose Ananias's desire of not wanting to help Saul see again. From a human perspective, it simply did not make sense to help Saul. Fortunately, God had the sensory attention of Ananias. Even though Ananias protested, he heard God tell him not to argue.

| *Uplifting* | *Discouraging* |
|---|---|
| ➢ | ➢ |
| ➢ | ➢ |
| ➢ | ➢ |

This is a valuable lesson for all of us. When we hear God's voice and he does not seem to make any sense, share your concerns with God. Let him know how you feel. David openly questioned God on many occasions in the Psalms. It is part of our sensory focus on God. If we don't keep our doubts to ourselves and stay stuck in our own thinking, God will respond to our protests and we will hear his response to our worries.

| *Uplifting* | *Discouraging* |
|---|---|
| ➢ | ➢ |
| ➢ | ➢ |
| ➢ | ➢ |

## *Stop Thinking!*

Ananias certainly listened to God after his initial protest. Look at the impact of Ananias's listening to God's voice on the conversion of Saul to Paul, the conversion of a man who went from his own hateful thinking about God to loving God's voice in the control center of his brain:

> *Saul spent a few days getting acquainted with the Damascus disciples, but then went right to work, wasting no time, preaching in the meeting places that this Jesus was the Son of God. They were caught off guard by this and, not at all sure they could trust him, they kept saying, "Isn't this the man who wreaked havoc in Jerusalem among the believers? And didn't he come here to do the same thing—arrest us and drag us off to jail in Jerusalem for sentencing by the high priests?"*
>
> *But their suspicions didn't slow Saul down for even a minute. His momentum was up now and he plowed straight into the opposition, disarming the Damascus Jews and trying to show them that this Jesus was the Messiah.* (Acts 9:19-22)

For me, the story of Saul's conversion to Paul is my favorite Bible example that describes the beauty of God's design for the human brain. It was not his own. There was no way a human could change himself from Saul who killed Jews to Paul who preached the Messiah. None of us, like Saul, are

| *Uplifting* | *Discouraging* |
|---|---|
| ➢ | ➢ |
| ➢ | ➢ |
| ➢ | ➢ |

capable of converting our own thinking. Saul could have spent decades in cognitive behavioral therapy and never converted his thoughts from hate to love. My desire is that all my clients and readers stop any and all efforts to convert their thinking from negative to positive. These efforts simply result in total frustration and more deeply-rooted negative thinking. Our thoughts can only be dealt with through supernatural, radical action by God. There is no such thing as converting our thoughts. They need total replacement by God. In this process of God becoming our voice, he doesn't remove our voice. God uses it to remind us how negative it is. Any guest appearances alert us to run back into God's arms.

| *Uplifting* | *Discouraging* |
|---|---|
| ➢ | ➢ |
| ➢ | ➢ |
| ➢ | ➢ |

## *Stop Trying So Hard*

I sincerely hope this book on the Bible and the Brain gives you a new desire to hear God's voice and have God's thinking replace your own thinking. I delight in the fact that God is so counterintuitive from the perspective of how he constructed the brain. I spent nearly a lifetime trying to figure out what God said in the Bible. When I learned, and accepted, that God never intended for my own thinking to figure out the Bible, only then was I able to grasp that God's Word meant the opposite of what seemed logical to me. God's Word is sensory-based, not logic-based. That is the whole reason for faith. Faith would not factor into the equation if the Bible was based on logic. Faith is not positive thinking. Faith is following God with our five senses, and not having a clue where he is taking us. We learn that when we follow God with sensory attention, he gives us love and happiness, despite our circumstances. God's love and happiness are the spiritual nourishment required by our brain for us to be the healthy children that God needs to share his message around the world.

I recently spoke to a Christian married couple who were being excruciatingly mean to each other. Each blamed their partner for their meanness and insisted I fix their spouse. They even accused each other of not being saved. I politely told them that their salvation was a private matter between them and God. I also told them they were not capable of having kind thoughts about each other and they should give up trying

| *Uplifting* | *Discouraging* |
|---|---|
| ➢ | ➢ |
| ➢ | ➢ |
| ➢ | ➢ |

to be nice. As expected, they both looked at me like I was from another planet.

I began to teach them that God never intended for us to be able to feel love and communicate our love in marriage on our own. I told them God did not make their brains with this ability. Of course, my advice is the opposite of what is taught in our culture and church. Unfortunately, most of us have been wrong our entire lives in our interpretation of what God says in his Word. It is only when we read the Bible through the eyes of how God made the brain can we see the sensory meaning of his instruction. God's instruction—in fact, God's voice—is always counterintuitive. That is one way we can tell it is God's voice. His thoughts are always the opposite of our human logic. Thankfully, we can always rely on God's thoughts and his voice to bring us love and happiness. All we have to do is devote our sensory attention to God.

---

| *Uplifting* | *Discouraging* |
|---|---|
| ➤ | ➤ |
| ➤ | ➤ |
| ➤ | ➤ |

## *God's Love is Electric*

My desire is that everyone gets a chance to read this book, especially pastors and church leaders who have never learned how God made the brain. It is not fair to expect them to have learned God's design and purpose for the human brain since our learning institutions at every level have not incorporated this teaching. However, all of us would benefit significantly from this learning. After all, God did make a brain for every one of us. What was God's primary purpose for giving each of us a brain? Without a doubt, his purpose was to design a way for us to experience his love to the sensory maximum and to share our experience of his love with others:

> *Just then a religion scholar stood up with a question to test Jesus. "Teacher, what do I need to do to get eternal life?"*
>
> *He answered, "What's written in God's Law? How do you interpret it?"*
>
> *He said, "That you love the Lord your God with all your passion and prayer and muscle and intelligence—and that you love your neighbor as well as you do yourself."*
>
> *"Good answer!" said Jesus. "Do it and you'll live."*
> (Luke 10:25-28)

| *Uplifting* | *Discouraging* |
|---|---|
| ➢ | ➢ |
| ➢ | ➢ |
| ➢ | ➢ |

Passion, prayer, muscle, and even intelligence are all sensory words. Love has nothing to do with our so-called thinking intelligence. Our thinking is passive, it is cursed. It serves no purpose except to create worry. When we tune in our five senses to God, he wills us with passion, sensory muscle, and emotional intelligence. What do I mean by sensory muscle and emotional intelligence? When we are connected to God through our five senses, we can hear his thoughts and words. His input is alive with passion and strength and intelligence. Only God's thinking on our behalf gives us intelligence when it comes to both logic and emotion. God's logic and emotion become so strong in us that it overpowers and silences our twisted thoughts and fear based emotions.

Only when we rely on God with our five senses can we receive and be filled with his love. Only God's love in us energizes us to love him with all our might. But be careful—this energy is also highly contagious! We are so electrically charged with his love that it is on display through us to all those around us (our neighbors). We cannot contain his love. God's love is explosive and shoots fireworks from us to anyone in our sphere of influence. God lights up the world through us:

| *Uplifting* | *Discouraging* |
|---|---|
| ➢ | ➢ |
| ➢ | ➢ |
| ➢ | ➢ |

*Remember, our Message is not about ourselves; we're proclaiming Jesus Christ, the Master. All we are is messengers, errand runners from Jesus for you. It started when God said, "Light up the darkness!" and our lives filled up with light as we saw and understood God in the face of Christ, all bright and beautiful.*

*If you only look at us, you might well miss the brightness. We carry this precious Message around in the unadorned clay pots of our ordinary lives.* (2 Corinthians 4:5-7)

| Uplifting | Discouraging |
|---|---|
| ➤ | ➤ |
| ➤ | ➤ |
| ➤ | ➤ |

| Uplifting | Discouraging |
|---|---|
| ➢ | ➢ |
| ➢ | ➢ |
| ➢ | ➢ |

## *God Lives in Us*

When we read in God's Word that "our Message is not about ourselves, we are proclaiming Jesus Christ," it is vitally important that we consider how God designed our brain. Because of how God made our brain, it is impossible to tune in and listen to our own thoughts and listen to God's voice at the same time. God doesn't want us to listen to our own thoughts. He desires that we are always tuned into his thoughts through our five senses. Being sensory with God silences our own thoughts. This is the brain mechanism that allows us to be errand runners or messengers from Jesus to others. By God's supernatural design, this is the only way for him to produce his love in us; and, for us to transport God's love to others. Love becomes the centerpiece of our lives, just as God intended.

Some of us have worked our tails off our entire lives in our futile attempt to love and be loved. All our mental efforts have been in vain because our own cursed thoughts produce only hate, not love. God made the human brain to love and be loved an entirely different way, counterintuitive to our own human thinking. In fact, the only way to live a life of love is to live a life in God's presence through sensory focus. The Bible tells us exactly how to live this life in him:

> *But if God himself has taken up residence in your life, you can hardly be thinking more of yourself than of him. Anyone, of course, who has not welcomed this invisible*

| *Uplifting* | *Discouraging* |
|---|---|
| ➤ | ➤ |
| ➤ | ➤ |
| ➤ | ➤ |

*but clearly present God, the Spirit of Christ, won't know what we're talking about. But for you who welcome him, in whom he dwells—even though you still experience all the limitations of sin—you yourself experience life on God's terms. It stands to reason, doesn't it, that if the alive-and-present God who raised Jesus from the dead moves into your life, he'll do the same thing in you that he did in Jesus, bringing you alive to himself? When God lives and breathes in you (and he does, as surely as he did in Jesus), you are delivered from that dead life. With his Spirit living in you, your body will be as alive as Christ's!* (Romans 8:9-11)

This scripture was always a mystery to me until God showed me how he designed our brain. I never knew how God took up residence in my life. I never knew how to focus on his thoughts instead of my own. I never knew how God could live and breathe in me or bring me to be alive in him. There is one simple answer to every one of these "I never knew" statements. The one and only answer is to be closely attached to God with our five senses—the point of entry to our brain. Down through the ages, our culture and church have consistently had the incorrect answers because they have looked at the brain design backwards. Our brain's point of entry is not our thinking side. It is our sensory side.

---

| *Uplifting* | *Discouraging* |
|---|---|
| ➢ | ➢ |
| ➢ | ➢ |
| ➢ | ➢ |

## *Don't Worry*

How can God possibly dwell in me while I still experience all the limitations of sin? How can I still experience life on God's terms? That was another mystery to me until I learned how God made the brain. When I sinned in the past, I felt too much guilt to even imagine God still dwelled in me. I was too ashamed to experience life on God's terms. With knowledge about how God made the brain, I have learned that God dwells in me through my sensory focus on him. God does not remove the limitation of sin. Nor does he remove the part of my brain that gives me the choice to sin. I still have the choice to think my own sinful thoughts. I still have the memories of my sinful thoughts. At any time, I can and sometimes do jump back into my own thinking. God made our brain so we will always have that choice.

God's desire is that we choose to keep the attention of our five senses on him. This simple choice to focus on God keeps our thoughts silent. When our own thoughts creep and even jump back in, God wants to use our own cursed thoughts as a prompt and vivid reminder to fix our sensory focus back on him. Fortunately, God designed this flip back to sensory focus on him not to require any mental effort on our part. It is just a turning of our eyes, a tuning in of our ears, a different touch, a fresh taste, or a fragrant smell. In other words, God made our brain in such a brilliant fashion that he uses our sinful nature to give us the desire to run away from sin into his loving

| *Uplifting* | *Discouraging* |
|---|---|
| ➢ | ➢ |
| ➢ | ➢ |
| ➢ | ➢ |

arms. He gives us a sensory escape from dwelling on our guilt and shame.

This is an example of how God's actual teaching is the opposite of what our culture and church have taught all these years. I was taught to dwell on my shame and guilt to self-motivate me to stop sinning. However, dwelling on my shame and guilt only kept me stuck in my own thoughts and drowning in my own sin. To learn God made my brain with such a simple way of sensory escape to him saved the day for me. God doesn't leave me when I sin. He does not turn his back on me. He is only a glance, a scent, a touch, a sound, or a flavor away. No, I am not new age, nor is this way of teaching. God just made my brain in such an amazing way that his presence in me and all around me remains solid and as sturdy as a rock:

> *Then Moses summoned Joshua. He said to him with all Israel watching, "Be strong. Take courage. You will enter the land with this people, this land that God promised their ancestors that he'd give them. You will make them the proud possessors of it. God is striding ahead of you. He's right there with you. He won't let you down; he won't leave you. Don't be intimidated. Don't worry."* (Deuteronomy 31:7-8)

---

| *Uplifting* | *Discouraging* |
|---|---|
| ➢ | ➢ |
| ➢ | ➢ |
| ➢ | ➢ |

## *Raised from the Dead*

One final mystery from Romans 6:9-11, where Paul wrote that God delivers us from a dead life just like he raised Jesus from the dead. These verses never had any meaning for me until I learned about how our brain works. These words always sounded poetic. How nice that Paul wrote words that sounded so good. But I was clueless about their interpretation. Learning about how God made the brain is critical to be able to interpret scripture accurately. Our cursed human thinking is not capable of accurate Bible translation. Only God's thoughts in our brain can accurately interpret God's Word. The correct interpretation by God (using his design for our brain) of delivering us from the dead is our five senses being brought to life in him.

Before we were rescued by God, our five senses were dead to him. We devoted the attention of our senses to false gods. These false gods included our own thinking and all the addictions to which our senses were glued. We devoted our attention to alcohol, drugs, porn, money, food, sex, clothes; the list goes on and on. These false gods drained all life from us. They killed our desire and sensory interest in God. We were numb to God. We could not see him or hear him. We even became numb to the sounds, smells, and tastes of God's creation. We experienced a sensory death. We were depressed, like a dead man walking. Our five senses lost their life. The stories of sensory death I have heard over and over again by

| *Uplifting* | *Discouraging* |
|---|---|
| ➢ | ➢ |
| ➢ | ➢ |
| ➢ | ➢ |

alcoholics and drug addicts have taken on new meaning since I have learned about how God made the brain. Alcohol and drugs literally kill brain cells. Our senses became dull and listless the more we abuse alcohol and drugs.

Even obsessive thoughts can dull our senses. A few years ago, I worked with a client who became so stuck in the thinking side of his brain he had difficulty tasting his favorite food, pizza. My client's overthinking hindered his ability to enjoy the flavors and aromas of food. If we don't take the time to enjoy the smell and taste of food, our memory area for those sensations becomes muted and tasteless. I helped my client overcome his problem by having him exaggerate the practice of smelling foods. When he took a bite of pizza, the focus of smell also helped him once again taste and enjoy his favorite food.

I am so thankful God designed the human brain the way he did. God made us with such resiliency. He breathes new life into us every day as we feast on him with our five senses. He gives us divine medication to lift our depression.

---

| *Uplifting* | *Discouraging* |
|---|---|
| ➤ | ➤ |
| ➤ | ➤ |
| ➤ | ➤ |

## *What a Surprise*

God's divine medication is intended to be used as an intravenous flow into our veins rather than a periodic popping of pills. God desires that our five senses tune into him on a continual basis. In FocusChoice language, we call this sensory prayer. The reference for sensory prayer in the Bible is "pray without ceasing." This biblical instruction never seemed possible to me until I learned about God's construction of the brain. I know I could never pray on a continual basis in the traditionally-taught way. However, God designed our brain so we can choose to have our five senses in continual, conscious contact with him. When anyone doubts this cerebral capability installed by God, I remind them of our un-Biblical ability to "worry without ceasing." God gave our brain the capacity to tune into his thoughts continuously rather than be tuned into our own worrisome thoughts. I also remind people of an addict's continual obsession with their addiction. Just as we are capable of constant attention to a self-destructive life, God desires that we use our brain capacity to give him our constant attention. Continual sensory prayer is an ongoing preoccupation and obsession to be in constant sensory contact with God rather than our false gods. Thankfully, there is no possibility of overdosing on God! The more deeply we stay in close sensory union with him, the more God brings to life his love in our lives.

---

| *Uplifting* | *Discouraging* |
|---|---|
| ➢ | ➢ |
| ➢ | ➢ |
| ➢ | ➢ |

Our sensory preoccupation with God is our only hope for not allowing our sinful thoughts to tell us what to do. Our sinful thoughts look for every opportunity to sneak back into the limelight in our brain. We are protected from our sinful thoughts only when we develop the practice of keeping God in our field of vision at all times:

> *But now that you've found you don't have to listen to sin tell you what to do, and have discovered the delight of listening to God telling you, what a surprise! A whole, healed, put-together life right now, with more and more of life on the way! Work hard for sin your whole life and your pension is death. But God's gift is real life, eternal life, delivered by Jesus, our Master.* (Romans 6:22-23)

These verses capture the story of my life! My guess is I have read these verses numerous times over the years. They just never jumped out at me until I found out how God made my brain.

---

*Uplifting*                                    *Discouraging*

➢                                              ➢

➢                                              ➢

➢                                              ➢

## *You Don't Have to Listen to Sin*

I was told my whole life I did not have to listen to sin tell me what to do. However, I never discovered the delight of listening to God telling me until I learned how to live a FocusChoice life. After all these years, it was truly a great surprise to me. What stood in the way of me learning how not to listen to sin? Even though these verses say working hard my whole life only yields a death pension, my cultural and church heritage taught me that I did not try hard enough. However, it seemed the harder I tried, the more I sinned. I was also taught I did not have enough desire to stop listening to sin. As a result, I felt I was lazy, or a fraud, or a loser.

The truth is I was lazy, and an imposter, and a loser. I still am! Nothing I think, say, or do can heal me and give me a whole, put-together life right now. It was revelational to learn God has never expected that from me. God did not make my brain so I could put my life together. God designed my brain so only he could put my life together. But how? For starters, I must accept my own inability to change. My thoughts are forever cursed. They are and always will be negative and hateful. They cannot be un-cursed. I never honestly accepted that truth before. I was correctly taught that my thoughts were the problem. But—surprise!—I always thought and was taught that my thoughts could be corrected.

| *Uplifting* | *Discouraging* |
|---|---|
| ➢ | ➢ |
| ➢ | ➢ |
| ➢ | ➢ |

My thoughts are incapable of correction. My thoughts are incapable of not listening to sin tell me what to do. My thoughts have to be replaced by God's thoughts. My voice has to be replaced by God's voice. Our brain was not designed to be able to listen to our thoughts and his thoughts at the same time. Our brain is not able to hear our own voice and God's voice simultaneously. Hearing his voice is the one and only secret to discovering the delight of listening to God telling me what to do. Somehow, that secret eluded me all these years. Until I learned God created our brain with a sensory side, I did not know how to listen to God. I did not know how to hear his voice. I did not even know how to read the Bible. These "how" answers have changed my life forever. God has shown me the delight of listening to him through simply tuning in my five senses to him and his Word. My desire is that reading this book will help you discover this delight!

---

*Uplifting*                                             *Discouraging*

➤                                              ➤


➤                                              ➤


➤                                              ➤

## *References*

1. Hampton, Debbie. (2016). *How Your Thoughts Change Your Brain, Cells and Genes.* Retrieved from http://www.huffingtonpost.com/debbie-hampton/how-your-thoughts-change-your-brain-cells-and-genes_b_9516176.html.

2. Jabr, Ferris. (2011). *Cache Cab: Taxi Drivers' Brains Grow to Navigate London's Streets.* Retrieved from https://www.scientificamerican.com/article/london-taxi-memory/.

3. Schwartz, Jeffrey M. (1997). *Brain Lock: Free Yourself from Obsessive-Compulsive Behavior.* New York, NY: Harper Perennial.

4. Siegel, Daniel J. (2010). *Mindsight: The New Science of Personal Transformation.* New York, NY: Bantam.

5. Seligman, Martin E. P., Walker, Elaine F., Rosenhan, David L. (2000). *Abnormal Psychology* (4th ed.). New York, NY: W. W. Norton & Company.

6. Graham, Billy. (2006). *Reading the Bible.* Retrieved from https://billygraham.org/decision-magazine/june-2006/reading-the-bible/.

7. Carey, Phillip. (20010). *Is This God's Voice or Mine?* Retrieved from http://www.relevantmagazine.com/god/deeper-walk/features/22657-is-this-gods-voice-or-mine.

8. Hamp, Bob. (2010). *Think Differently Live Differently: Keys to a Life of Freedom.* Dallas, TX: Thinking Differently Press.

9. BrainHQ. (2016). *Your Brain in Love.* Posit Science. Retrieved from http://www.brainhq.com/brain-resources/brain-facts-myths/brain-in-love.

10. Fischer. Helen. (2008). *Your Brain in Love.* Retrieved from https://www.ted.com/talks/helen_fisher_studies_the_brain_in_love.

# Scripture Index

**Genesis**
3:17-19 ..................... 110

**Deuteronomy**
31:7-8 ....................... 225

**1 Kings**
19:11-12 ..................... 131

**Nehemiah**
8:10 ............................ 94

**Psalm**
107:10-16 ................... 165
119:25-32 ..................... 53
23:4-6 .......................... 74
34:4-8 .......................... 75
35:9-10 ........................ 42
51:1-10 ...................... 197
51:11-15 .................... 200
51:16-17 .................... 202
55:16-18 .................... 115
6:6-10 ........................ 147
61:1-2 ........................ 150
61:3-5 .................. 49,151
63:6-8 .......................... 43
69:13-18 .................... 153
69:29 ......................... 156
69:30-36 .................... 156
71:17-20 .................... 157
8:1-3,9 ....................... 146
84:10-11 ...................... 43
86:1-7 .......................... 37
9:1-2 ............................ 42
91:14-16 ...................... 52
119:105 .......................... i

**Proverbs**
3:5-8 ............................ 59
4:20-22 ........................ 99
4:25-27 ........................ 99

**Isaiah**
43:2-4 .......................... 48
46:3-4 .......................... 58
55:6-9 ........................ 108
64:6 ........................... 129

**Jeremiah**
1:5-8 .......................... 132

**Ezekiel**
36:25-27 ...................... 96

**Matthew**
11:28-30 ............... vi,49,78
18:1-5 ........................ 166

**Luke**
10:25-28 .................... 218
10:27 ......................... 137
11:33-34 ........................ i

**John**
1:5-9 ............................. i
8:12 .............................. i
10:1-5 ........................ 161
10:19-21 .................... 161
3:16-18 ...................... 102

**Acts**
13:22 ........................... 61
7:54-60 ...................... 208
9:11-12 ...................... 211
9:13-15 ...................... 212
9:1-6 .......................... 209

9:19-22 .......................... 214
9:7-9 .............................. 210

**Romans**
12:1-2 ............................ 84
12:6-8 ............................ 82
3:10-16 .......................... 191
5:5 .................................. 204
6:6-14 ............................ 139
6:22-23 .......................... 229
7:14-16 .......................... 89
7:17-25 .......................... iii
8:29 ................................ 3
8:34-39 .......................... 184
8:5-6 .............................. 47
8:9-11 ............................ 222

**1 Corinthians**
2:7-9 .............................. 36
7:32,35 .......................... 120
9:24-27 .......................... 79

**2 Corinthians**
1:4 .................................. 206
10:5-6 ............................ 27
12:6-12 .......................... 174
4:5-7 .............................. 220
5:14-20 .......................... 104

**Galatians**
3:1-3 .............................. 97
5:19-21 .......................... 56
5:19-23 .......................... 116
5:22-23 .......................... 57

**Ephesians**
2:1-6 .............................. 32
2:7-10 ............................ 70
3:14-19 .......................... 195
3:20 ................................ 48
4:14-16 .......................... 170
4:22-24 .......................... 15
4:24 ................................ 95
4:26-27 .......................... 61
5:1-2 .............................. 95

**Philippians**
1:6 .................................. 65
2:12-13 .......................... 68
2:1-4 .............................. 103
4:10-13 .......................... 43
4:6-7 .............................. 62
4:8 .................................. 5
4:8-9 .............................. 46

**Colossians**
1:11-12 .......................... 98
1:21-23 .......................... 205
3:12-14 .......................... 135

**Hebrews**
12:1-3 ............................ 34
12:2 ................................ 123

**1 Peter**
4:12-16 .......................... 142

**2 Peter**
3:9 .................................. 69

**1 John**
4: 17-19 ......................... 193
4:7-10 ............................ 207

## *About the Author*

David Heebner, LPC, has had a broad and successful career of more than 30 years working in the field of mental healthcare; from helping individual clients with clinical or behavioral addiction issues to running treatment centers that aid people in recovering from addictions of all kinds. Currently, David manages his own private practice in northern Virginia. He provides outpatient services to individuals, couples, parents, and children from his offices in Chantilly and Ashburn, and worldwide via FaceTime. In 2012, David began to develop the FocusChoice Therapy model, which draws on spiritual principles and neuroscientific discoveries to bring peace and freedom to people who live imprisoned by performance-based thinking. He is also the author of *Clear My Vision: A Year of Focus on Christ* and *Heavenly Addiction: Overcoming Earthly Addictions God's Way*.